Waldorf Kindergartens Today

Waldorf Kindergartens Today

Edited by Peter Lang *and* Marie-Luise Compani

Floris Books

Translated by Matthew Barton

First published in German under the title
Waldorfkindergarten heute by Verlag Freies Geistesleben 2011
First published in English by Floris Books 2013

British Library CIP data available
ISBN 978-178250-018-6
Printed in Poland

Contents

Foreword

In December 1899, when the Swedish parliament gathered for its final session of the nineteenth century, the teacher, journalist and MP Ellen Key gave a widely praised speech. She said that the coming twentieth century must be the century of the child, and sketched out a future education system that would acknowledge and assure the rights of children as autonomous individuals. She highlighted children's innate capacity to learn and educate themselves, and the resulting need for educational institutions that took account of and facilitated such processes of self-education. Finally she suggested that societies failing to place children's fundamental rights and needs at the centre of their efforts would ultimately collapse or at least suffer severely.

A few years later, in 1907, Maria Montessori opened her first 'children's house' in Rome. A key principle of Montessori's educational ideas is summed up in the phrase, 'Help me to do it myself!' Montessori voiced this appeal to all parents, educators and educational policy makers on behalf of the world's children. Instead of presenting children with a ready-made world, Maria Montessori wanted to offer them a reality they could increasingly engage with, understand and learn to shape through their own activity, experiences and perceptions.

At the beginning of the same year, Rudolf Steiner gave a series of lectures on education in Berlin, which were published in the spring of 1907 as *The Education of the Child in the Light of Spiritual Science*. In the introduction to this volume he wrote:

> It is not my aim to call for particular measures or establish programmes but simply to describe the nature of the child. The nature of the growing human being himself will lead in a quite self-evident way to perspectives that inform education.[1]

In the course of the same book, Steiner takes the reader on a voyage of discovery, studying the child's visible physical body, as well as other invisible aspects that education can develop: for example, the child's life forces, feelings and sensations, and a sense of self that increasingly emerges, unfolds and changes over time. Steiner dismisses a merely materialistic view of the human being along with the forms of education geared to this, instead highlighting the multi-level, changing phases, stages and processes of development and transformation that occur in every child.

By the start of the twenty-first century, however, children's rights to their own childhood have still not been assured, despite binding United Nations commitments to human rights in general, and endorsement of a UN Convention on the Rights of the Child. It is true that many children attend nurseries and schools, live in decent houses, have enough to eat, receive good medical care and grow up in safe, loving circumstances. Nevertheless, far too many of them live in a world without underlying meaning, and their individual development is suppressed or hindered. Children are surrounded by violence, selfishness, egotism and indifference. Their love of movement is constrained, their imagination manipulated and disappointed, and frequently they fail to develop their full potential for speech and language. Many children suffer from stress, nervousness, anxiety, hearing damage, sleep disorders and allergies. And if we look at the countless crisis regions in the world, we find far more grievous plights: hunger, exploitation, persecution, a complete lack of education, and physical, psychological and spiritual oppression.

All the articles in this book seek to highlight children's primary and fundamental needs, as the basis for an educational approach that develops meaning and health. The authors identify risks to child development, including the dangers of 'accelerated education' in early childhood ('the quicker the better'), an ever earlier start to formal schooling, and its infiltration into nurseries. They describe wholesome alternatives to this, governed neither by modernity per se, nor unthinking perpetuation of the status quo.

A few years ago, Nelson Mandela was asked to give a speech at the opening of a centre for Steiner-Waldorf education in a South African township. Mandela described the educational task like this:

> A society's character is nowhere more apparent than in how it engages with children. Our success must be measured in our children's happiness and the way they flourish. In every society they are both its most vulnerable citizens and its richest resource.

Marie-Luise Compani
Peter Lang

I

Waldorf Kindergartens Today

Waldorf Kindergartens Around the World

Peter Lang

The Founding of the Waldorf School

Less than a year after World War I ended, the first Waldorf School was founded in Stuttgart in September 1919. It was the initiative of Emil Molt (1876–1936), the proprietor and founder of the Waldorf Astoria cigarette factory, who asked Rudolf Steiner (1861–1925) to establish a school and curriculum for the children of his factory workers. From the very outset, though, the Waldorf School opened its doors to children from all social classes, not just workers' children. And it was not an isolated phenomenon but part of the whole context of Steiner's social and political endeavours at the time, his commitment to a renewal of society. After the defeat of the 'Central Powers' in World War I and the collapse of the social order in Germany, new political impulses and proposals for state reform were sorely needed. Steiner's suggestion of a 'threefold social organism' envisaged separation between the three social domains of culture, law and rights, and economy. The state itself would be democratically organised and restricted to the domain of law and rights, while the economy and cultural life would be self-administrated by independent bodies. The origins of the Waldorf School must be seen in this context: schooling, as a key element of culture, was to develop quite independently of state controls.

The main features of Steiner-Waldorf education, as Steiner conceived them in 1919, and as they have emerged and developed over time, have been described in detail in other publications.[2] They take into account of the needs of the whole child – academic, physical, emotional and spiritual – balancing the development of intellectual, artistic, craft and practical abilities. The curriculum for formal schooling extends over twelve years, from rising seven to the age of eighteen, during which a stable learning community forms, unhampered by recourse to grades or formal exams. The educational content is geared to children's inner development and their age-specific needs, rather than to external requirements or economic interests imposed upon schools.

The development of Waldorf kindergartens

At the beginning of the twentieth century, Rudolf Steiner recognised that daily life was increasingly at odds with the nature of children, and that traditions of upbringing and education were fast disappearing. He felt that Waldorf education should also cater for pre-school children. We can see this from two statements he made about the founding of the Waldorf School:

> Mainly we admit children in the same way as they enter ordinary primary schools. We can start teaching once the age of imitation has passed. But it would be very good to introduce some things in the first seven years as well.*
>
> And:
>
> I have always found it especially painful that at the Waldorf School in Stuttgart we do not get children until they have reached the designated age in Central Europe for the start of formal schooling.[3]

*In Germany the starting age for formal schooling is between six and seven.

But it was not until 1926, after Steiner's death, that Elisabeth Grunelius started a Waldorf kindergarten and incorporated it into the first Waldorf School in Stuttgart. Subsequently a few kindergartens were founded in other cities. The further growth of the kindergarten movement was prevented after the banning of Waldorf education by the Nazis in 1933, and the outbreak of World War II. At the end of the war, a group of kindergarten teachers and physicians formed around the Waldorf educationalist Klara Hattermann in Hanover, and formulated a methodology for kindergarten and parent advisory work based on Steiner's insights into child development. From then on the number of Waldorf kindergartens rose continually.

At the end of the 1950s and the beginning of the 1960s, the protected space of early childhood was increasingly at risk in many countries. In 1956 the Soviet Union became the first country to successfully launch a satellite into orbit. This technical achievement triggered a shock wave in the western world with consequences not only for the military and economic domains but also for views about education. Western countries sought to catch up with the Soviet Union's technological head start by pursuing increasingly one-sided educational policies. In pre-school years an emphasis arose on cultivating children's cognitive development through formal learning, such as literacy and numeracy skills.

But a social counter-movement also arose at this time, as university students tried to disrupt fixed authoritarian structures. From 1968, ideas of human emancipation from social and political constraints grew to be a generally accepted educational and developmental goal.

Waldorf educationalists were very active during this phase of intense transformation of the educational landscape. There was a boom in new Waldorf schools in Germany. Parents and teachers demonstrated radical commitment, and it became apparent that early years development and education must likewise be approached from a fundamentally new angle. Figures of note here were the experienced German Waldorf educationalists Klara Hattermann in Hanover and Freya Jaffke in Reutlingen, as well as the Stuttgart Waldorf teacher Dr Helmut von Kuegelchen.

On 19 October, 1969, as the fruition of many years' intense collaboration with the Waldorf Schools Association and teachers involved in it, the International Association of Waldorf Kindergartens was founded. Those present on this occasion report that the founding members could fit comfortably into a single classroom. The pioneers set to work, engaging in debates on educational policy, organising educational conferences, supporting the many initiatives to found Waldorf kindergartens worldwide, and developing a network of international contacts.

With the collapse of the Iron Curtain, a further wave of new kindergartens arose in former Eastern Bloc countries from 1990 onwards. After the first decade of the twenty-first century, there were around 1,600 Waldorf kindergartens and mother and toddler groups in over fifty countries around the world, and the concept is spreading continually. Currently there is increasing interest in Waldorf education in Southeast Asia, where kindergartens, schools and training courses are also being established.

Idea into action: How to found a Waldorf kindergarten?

Here I would like to add some basic information about founding a Waldorf kindergarten, to help guide parents who may wish to do this.

You will need a group of people with the same aim. The impetus for starting a new kindergarten often comes from parents who are looking for a different educational approach from those they find in their neighbourhood, or who can find no available place for their child in an existing Waldorf kindergarten.

In recent years, Waldorf kindergartens have also been founded by committed individuals in socially disadvantaged areas of various cities, with the aim of nurturing social and educational initiatives there and reaching children who wouldn't otherwise seek out Waldorf education. In Mannheim, Germany, such an initiative gave rise to the Free Intercultural Waldorf School.

In the UK, the current government's programme to help fund 'free schools' of all kinds is also leading to increasing applications for support for new Waldorf schools, thus hopefully making them more widely available in multi-cultural settings. For some years there has been government funding for fifteen hours of nursery provision per week for three and four-year-olds, which has benefited Waldorf kindergartens.

Once a founding group has formed, whose members are able to commit to realising this aim for as long as needed, they should seek contact with Waldorf kindergartens in the local area. Open days, festivals, public talks and books also provide a good opportunity to become further acquainted with Waldorf education.

Waldorf kindergartens are affiliated with each other in regional or national groups, and a new initiative can look to these groups for advice and support for their next steps. If the initiative gathers momentum, a time will come to find an appropriate legal form, usually as an officially recognised association. For this you will need a constitution, an executive and association members. Local Waldorf kindergartens and their administrative bodies will have experience of this and can offer support.

The new association will also need to publicise itself in the local community and area. The search for premises, or land where a Waldorf kindergarten can be built, likewise, requires a good deal of work. A Waldorf kindergarten teacher will also need to be found.

If all those involved work together well, a new Waldorf kindergarten or nursery can start – with further efforts needed, of course, to ensure that development proceeds in a strong, healthy way.

The international association for Steiner-Waldorf Early Childhood Education

The Waldorf kindergarten movement is now active throughout the world. It supports, stimulates and initiates efforts to ensure that the care and education of young children from birth through to school age becomes a national and international concern. In doing so it cooperates with Waldorf school movements. The international association of Waldorf kindergartens (now called the International Association for Steiner-Waldorf Early Childhood Education, or IASWECE) has set itself the task of supporting the spread of Waldorf education worldwide, and of nurturing professional dialogue between Waldorf kindergarten teachers. Twice a year, member country representatives meet as an international council to report on current projects, such as Waldorf training and professional development, the founding of new kindergartens, and to prepare international conferences. All these and other tasks require not only commitment but also funding, which comes from each respective country or from the mutual solidarity group of member countries.

Due to the enormous growth of the Waldorf kindergarten movement, it formed its own independent charitable association in 2005, with headquarters in Stockholm. The national and international tasks of the movement have changed little over the years: current obstacles and threats to child development are comparable with the situation forty years ago. However, the so-called PISA studies have, in part, brought with them a renewed wave of changes and restrictions.

PISA and its consequences

In most of the 32 OECD (Organisation for Economic Co-operation and Development) countries, the PISA studies (Programme for International Student Assessment) that commenced in 2000 are now carried out in a three-year cycle. Using standardised tests, these studies carry out international performance comparisons between fifteen-year-old students. Germany has performed comparatively poorly in these studies so far, which has led to contention in debates on education policy and calls for an earlier start to formal schooling. Yet a study published in 2005 by Darmstadt Technical University on 'The effect of school starting age on pupil performance' produced the following result:

> Children who, in line with current policies start formal schooling at around age 6.5 instead of six or earlier, gain long-term advantage from this. The greater maturity of older reception pupils leads to them having a considerably better understanding of reading texts by the end of primary schooling (after four years) and they are therefore more likely to go to a Gymnasium [grammar school]. In the light of these findings, a policy that keeps bringing the start of formal schooling forward seems of questionable benefit[...][4]

In Germany, this debate has created more public awareness of the importance of children's pre-school development. At present, therefore, there are excellent opportunities for Waldorf education to engage with these issues and present its own models and views of early childhood in a way that can affect state education policies in Germany.

The limited use and value of the comparative PISA studies has also become apparent. Different countries, for instance, with top rankings on the list, have completely different educational methods and approaches. In one of the 'top' countries, children start formal schooling early and take a strong cognitive approach in kindergarten, whereas in others the children stay a year longer in kindergarten and have opportunities to develop their aptitudes in extensive periods of free play. It seems doubtful whether the performance of completely different education systems can be evaluated using criteria such as the standardised ones of the

OECD. After all, certain human gifts, inclinations and capacities such as imagination, love of play or social skills can scarcely be measured and certainly not recorded in tests. Nor indeed *should* they be recorded. There is likely to be a general consensus that childhood education is not just a matter of content, of *what* is taught, but the quality of *how* this happens.

The right to childhood – a global challenge

Childhood does not happen by itself, but must always be created by each individual, by all of us. It is a cultural task and achievement to give space to childhood. It took a long span of human history before childhood came to be seen as a separate phase of life and development, which needs protecting, nurturing and shaping. This task is one we need to keep tackling in future.

Much has been done in some countries – though not all by any means – to increase the protection and well-being of young children. There are no grounds, however, to be satisfied with what has already been achieved. Wherever possible, the International Association for Steiner-Waldorf Early Childhood Education will continue to collaborate with other organisations to ensure that children's fundamental right to their childhood becomes an ever-increasing reality.

The Challenge for Waldorf Early Years Care Today

Marie-Luise Compani

The unmistakeable call for early learning

Never before in Germany has there been such wide and prolonged debate about early years education and learning. The repercussions of the PISA trial and its findings at the beginning of the twenty-first century have led to new views in politics and society of pre-school children. What has changed and why? Further justified questions follow from this: is childhood always only viewed through the lens of new scientific findings, outlooks and methods or are there constants in childhood development? If so, how and where are these considered?

Changes in society over recent decades have had a significant effect on the way children are cared for. Changes to women's and men's lifestyles, in particular the roles of mothers and fathers, along with increasingly flexible working hours, have led to fundamental revisions in the care of the young and elderly. Parents look for suitable childcare, adapted to suit their specific needs and family arrangements.

Only 25 years ago in Germany, children were not considered ready for nursery school until the age of three. From the beginning of the 1990s, early years childcare provision increased, along with new parent initiatives such as playgroups and mother and toddler groups, gradually widening to cater for children under the age of three. Public interest has therefore repeatedly focused on the expansion of childcare facilities, and high expectations of the quality of care, education and learning for young children.

These new views derive on the one hand from scientific findings in the field of brain research. It has been shown that young children's capacity to learn and absorb is accentuated at certain phases of development (called 'developmental windows'). On the other hand, ever more negative findings in studies on children starting school have shown a clear increase in developmental delays, as well as speech, movement and concentration disorders, which render learning and lesson participation difficult or even impossible. This presents new tasks, above all, for early years professionals.

Childcare centres are now no longer regarded as mere childcare facilities, but, in current education policies, are tasked with being places of learning – although one can ask whether they were not already doing this. These new measures, however, make it clear that education does not just start with school but happens from birth and has a decisive influence on later development. Early childhood thus acquires a new significance and value. The poet Jean Paul (1763–1825) who wrote an educational book entitled *Levana or the Doctrine of Education*, put this very clearly when he wrote: 'A globetrotter will learn more from his wet-nurse in infancy than from all his travels put together.'[5] In saying this he was highlighting the fact that young children learn most intensively and formatively during this period, acquiring a foundation for their later life.

The educationalist Gerd Schaefer promotes this view in his curriculum proposal entitled 'Education begins at birth'.[6] Young children bring with them the will and motivation to appropriate the world, to grasp, master and explore it – all at their own tempo and rhythm. They learn from the example of adults, their surroundings and the world. How these affect them, though, is the decisive thing. Does the adult world actually offer anything exemplary? What do the child's surroundings offer? And how do infants experience the world through their own explorations and 'incorporate' them?

Supporting people to become self-reliant and socially conscious is a generally valid goal in child and adolescent education. In the process of becoming an individual, learning to respect others and developing social skills, a person can progress towards freedom and responsibility.

Children entrusted to us in childcare centres bring with them their own stories, their cultural and family backgrounds. We can therefore ask about the nature of collaboration with children's families. How can parents and nurseries enter into fruitful dialogue to support a child's well-being? Where is help, support and supervision both necessary and useful? The inclusion of parents in the common education and learning process appears to be a further goal within educational provision (see also the essay by Claudia Grah-Wittich).

Here we find a further task for early years carers. They observe and accompany the child's learning process, document it in many ways, and also involve parents – for instance in annual discussions about the child's progress.

Developmental delays in individual children, such as speech impediments and remedial needs, should be detected early, allowing geared support to be given before formal schooling starts. The transition between kindergarten and school is an especially sensitive time for children and needs the full attention of parents and teachers, who should address it together.

In recent years, educationalists have also increasingly discussed the fact that girls often outshine boys. Generally, the former are more ambitious, more accommodating and successful, learning faster and on average achieving higher grades in their school-leaving exams. This throws up a whole raft of questions: Are our educational measures, already in early childhood, primarily informed or determined by women or female elements? What factors may disadvantage boys in kindergarten and school? Do to boys generally need a different educational approach from girls?[7] And what would this mean for educational work in the early years?

All in all we need a diverse range of ways to oversee childhood development, to study and nurture it. Naturally this also means new tasks for teachers, schools and families.

Therefore we may ask how early years care can best be organised to accommodate all of the tasks involved, and how such goals can be realised in practice. Does the drive to more formal learning leave enough scope for children to fulfil their most intrinsic need of play? What does learning mean, and how does the early learning process occur? And what demands does this make of Waldorf kindergarten pedagogy in relation to fulfilling core curricula?

These are gripping questions and tasks for teachers, parents and schools.

Waldorf kindergartens: new provisions, new tasks

A few years ago, only half-day groups were available in numerous Steiner-Waldorf kindergartens, where it was believed that young children develop best within a family context. No doubt this is generally desirable – as long as parents or the wider family can manage it. But the fact that, in a post-industrial society, work, training and childcare can go together, also has repercussions for the provision offered by Waldorf kindergartens and for the structure of their groups. These social developments require us to integrate anthroposophy and Waldorf education into the realities of life. By developing new outlooks, we can offer children space for healthy development despite any negative factors that may affect them.

For a good many years now, such changes have been taking place. Waldorf kindergartens now offer whole day and infant care, extended provision (such as 'afternoon care'), provision for children at transition age and a wealth of playgroups and mother and child groups – the latter particularly addressing the first three years. In disadvantaged areas of Germany integrative groups and childcare centres work with children and families from immigrant backgrounds.

Waldorf education regards one of its main emphases as developing a relationship and connection with children and their families. Since Waldorf childcare centres are managed independently and are oriented to specific needs, social environments and structures, the provision of group and individual care is, accordingly, geared to specific individual needs and circumstances.

Pre-school Education: Salutogenesis and Competency Development

Peter Lang

Every modern educational approach inevitably has to engage with other academic or scientific disciplines, such as neurobiology, the social sciences, psychology and medicine. It is therefore self-evident that the methodology and educational principles of Steiner-Waldorf schools and kindergartens stand in lively dialogue with other disciplines in the context of research and comparative studies. Waldorf education does not take place in a 'separate world' but stands fully within its surrounding societies and cultures, helping to shape them and serving contemporary needs. Here, therefore, I wish to describe two modern medical and psychological research institutes, and their connection with pre-school Waldorf provision.

Resilience research and education

The nuclear disasters at Chernobyl in 1986 and in Fukushima in 2011 had a devastating impact on the outlook of Europeans, deepening their concerns about threats to life in modern society. They became aware overnight of the dangers our contemporary civilisation produces. A book by Ulrich Beck was published in the same year as Chernobyl, and described generalised risks to life and development in modern societies. Beck describes risks, on the one hand, as resulting from a civilisation that practises global environmental destruction, and on the other he draws attention to:

> the risks of modern lifestyle as consequence of an enforced process of individualisation in modern societies, compelling individuals to shape their own biography and, in this regard, having to make decisions that carry permanent risk and find individual grounds for such decisions.[8]

On the 'plus side', this means a degree of self-determination never previously known, but on the 'risk side', people are exposed to radical changes such as global mass unemployment, poverty and devastating epidemics, such as Aids, which have direct impact on children and adolescents.

This is where resilience research comes into play. The term 'resilience' in humanities disciplines describes our general capacity to cope successfully with stressful realities, to bounce back rather than succumbing to misfortune and failures. In this context two fundamental questions arise in relation to child development and education:

- What strengths, basic skills and competencies help children develop in the healthiest way as regards body, psyche and social adjustment – irrespective of risks that may arise?
- How can we strengthen these powers of resistance through education?

We will return to these two questions later when we describe specific aspects of Waldorf education (see p.85). The second field of research, on 'salutogenesis', is concerned with a similar domain.

Salutogenesis – how health arises

Physicians and psychologists have always been concerned with curing and alleviating illnesses, and it is certain that they accomplish outstanding work in this field. The focus here is almost always on the patient, the sick person. However, one of the most influential psychologists of the twentieth century, Abraham Maslow (1908–1970) turned this view on its head at the beginning of the 1960s: starting from the observation that healthy people are scarcely ever the subject of research, he began to investigate the nature of health in studies on healthy subjects. At the same time, he was treating severely traumatised people who had survived the hell of German concentration camps between 1933 and 1945. He found that many of these patients did not have an especially robust physical constitution, but had tried during their terrible ordeal to access spiritual, artistic, religious, spiritual and social values, finding strength and endurance in these. In his efforts to discover the nature of health, Maslow noticed that the healthy subjects were 'very different, and in some respects surprisingly different, from the average'.[9]

According to Maslow, traits of healthy people commonly included the following:

- They possess a better perception of reality.
- They can accept themselves, others and nature.
- They have a natural simplicity and spontaneity.
- They are self-reliant and active.
- They possess authentic esteem; in other words, they value fundamental qualities and regard them with reverence, pleasure and wonder.
- They have a sense of community and commonality.
- They have a democratic character structure.
- They have a strongly ethical outlook.
- Their humour is philosophical rather than combative.
- Healthy people are, without exception, creative.[10]

It is clear that this range of positive human qualities and modes of conduct can be illuminating in relation to educational objectives and methods, and we will return to this theme later (see p.48).

One of Maslow's successors was the sociologist Aaron Antonovsky (1923–1994), today regarded as the 'father of salutogenesis'. Antonovsky's general criticism of traditional medical thinking takes issue with its assumption that pathogenic factors – those that make us sick – should be avoided or combated, while scarcely considering health-promoting – salutogenetic – powers. Both, he says, belong together. A small example by Eckhard Schiffer can show us what is involved here:

> Do you recall how it was? Lounging languorously in bed and excused all duties including homework. Mother caring for you, and dry rusks to eat (ah well!). Limeflower tea with honey – and being read to. So comforting and comfortable to have the flu. Or in other words: many healthy forces within us and around us that let us know we are not left alone and helpless to deal with the illness.[11]

The pathogenic factors – in this case the flu virus and soaking wet feet – are balanced by the health-sustaining or health-renewing factors: loving care, the sense of safety and protection, being read to, freedom to relax.

The core of Antonovsky's salutogenetic approach has three aspects, which we can regard as the basis of a healthy or health-recuperating human outlook:

- Comprehensibility – our capacity to see the interconnected contexts of the world.
- Manageability – or the capacity to gain trust in our growing self-reliance so that we cope well with our tasks in life, by our own powers or with the help of others.
- Meaningfulness – or the capacity to see our own thinking and way of life as having purpose, and acting accordingly.

These three aspects of a healthy or health-giving way of life, and ways to realise it, give rise to what Antonovsky calls a feeling and sense of coherence. We experience ourselves as embedded in an inner context and can therefore better engage with the outer world's multi-layered contexts. If we manage to know and govern ourselves, and be actively engaged in the world, this exerts a health-giving impetus. In other words, this human capacity to perceive and know ourselves and the world we live in, to shape our own meaning and experience inner security, means that we have a greater chance of becoming physically, psychologically and socially healthier.

The feeling of coherence thus indicates a basic mood of security, of being inwardly stable and consistent rather than collapsing, and at the same time allows us to find support and security in our connections with others. The sense of coherence describes a worldview associated with this feeling:

> My world is comprehensible, inwardly consistent, ordered. I can understand the problems and stresses that I experience as part of a wider context of meaning.
>
> Life confronts me with tasks that I can solve. I possess inner and outer resources which I can use to ably manage my life and cope with my current problems.
>
> Exertion and effort are meaningful in my life. There are goals and projects that are worth committing myself to.[12]

Waldorf pedagogy – a health-giving educational approach

In this context of resilience and salutogenesis research we can ask what health-giving characteristics can be found in Waldorf education and in the view of the human being on which it is founded. Before I examine specific educational measures and methodologies, I will highlight a few aspects of Waldorf pedagogy that are intrinsic to its underlying concept of the human being and important in relation to issues of resilience and salutogenesis research. What follows is drawn from findings by a Swiss research group directed by Thomas Marti in Bern, Switzerland.[13]

An extended view of the senses

Rudolf Steiner developed a unique view of the senses based on the idea that we have twelve senses. These are the basis for our healthy relationship with our own corporeality, our natural surroundings and our social milieu. The four 'lower' senses (sense of touch, life, our own movement, and balance) allow us to perceive our own body. The four 'middle' senses (smell, taste, vision, warmth) and the four 'upper' senses (hearing, speech, thought and sense of I or self) lead us to perceive the outer world and the inner nature of other people.[14]

A threefold view of the human being

Waldorf education is based on a threefold view of the human being: both psychologically, through thinking, feeling and will, and physiologically, through the organs of the neurosensory system, rhythmic system and metabolic/limb system. In highlighting the manifold correlations existing across these systems, Steiner distances himself from the view that psychology is merely a function of nerve processes and the nervous system. In terms of actual methodology, for Waldorf education this means that every process of learning draws not just on the brain and nervous system, but always also the whole human being.

A biographically-oriented psychophysiology of child development

Child development can be described in biographical phases marked, for instance, by second dentition and changes at puberty. At every phase children pass through characteristic and developmentally-necessary learning processes and steps. This view of life phases should, however, never be seen schematically, but taken as general guidance with different individual nuances for each child.

The Waldorf approach to pedagogy gives serious attention to psychological processes of development, and allows them the necessary time and space to unfold so that they can properly mature. It is for this reason that Waldorf education is opposed to one-sided development in the early years or harmful hot-housing. It seeks instead to help children develop in a physically, psychologically/spiritually and socially stable way, so that, as adolescents and adults, they can cope better with the demands of contemporary society.

A pedagogical ethos

Thus Waldorf pedagogy believes that it has a contribution to make to our whole culture, over and above an educational task geared only to the needs of society, although these are of course included. The prime focus is on responsibility to human nature itself, and this informs the pedagogical ethos of nursery carers and teachers. Children should be allowed to unfold the full individual potential of their gifts and capacities so that later they can contribute these to the enrichment and progress of society and culture.

This is only likely to succeed in an atmosphere in which those involved – parents, carers and teachers – seek a basic consensus regarding education.

Education for freedom

A health-giving form of pedagogy can unfold its positive effects where it is allowed to operate freely. The findings of the PISA study referred to above (see p.18) have shown (for instance in relation to the Finnish education system) that pleasure in creativity,

a sense of responsibility and motivation amongst carers, parents, teachers and, not least, pupils, are particularly high – giving rise to optimum identification with the educational process – where there is least external interference. A free cultural life, not dictated or constrained from above, is a major health-giving factor for all involved.

Childhood means time to play

Children come into the world as individuals who develop with their own gifts, inclinations, interests and also difficulties, and seek to go their own way. Education therefore always starts with observing children rather than judging them. As Rudolf Steiner said, 'The nature of the growing human being himself will give rise as though by itself to perspectives that inform education.'[15]

To shape this process as well as possible, children need competent adult models, loving and safe relationships and their own time to develop. As long ago as 1815, the great Swiss pedagogue Heinrich Pestalozzi wrote that, 'Education is example and love, and nothing other!'

Children should not therefore be squeezed into adult timetables nor made to accommodate adults' political or economic goals. Children are willing and happy to learn, and do so easily. Their 'developmental windows' are wide open, especially in the early years and the first years of school. We are responsible for shaping their worlds in a way that allows them to develop healthily.

The way in which children play reveals their current developmental stage and relationship to their surroundings on the one hand, and also, on the other, their capacity to relate to the world through actions, feelings and thinking. Human will and the urge for activity becomes apparent in babies, already, as they raise their heads, learn to support themselves on their arms, begin to sit and keep practising these things until they can stand and take their first steps. This urge to be active informs play in the first few years of life. Children immediately convert whatever they perceive through their senses into activity. This gives rise to play that is still largely non-goal oriented, often involving pleasure in repetition. Giving enough scope to this urge for movement and activity helps create the foundation we need as adults to engage our full will in dynamic action.

At the second stage of play, roughly between the ages of three and five, imagination joins the urge for activity. The child's imagination, one can say, creates the world anew, reshapes it, so that what is perceived through the senses is now incorporated into inner movement, reshaped in feeling and playfully reconfigured. Here the ground is prepared for the adult's later creative activity.

Roughly between five and seven, a third quality comes to the fore: powers of thought and understanding now increasingly imbue children's play, their powers of memory develop strongly and they mature into social beings. Children start to organise shared play, developing rules, planning things and making agreements. Sometimes they also form a kind of oppositional alliance against adults. Their mastery of language grows and they discover their own infinite expressive capacities, while observing their surroundings in increasingly precise and detailed ways. This third quality of children's play prepares our later capacity to gain clear, conceptual insight into the world and its interconnections.

None of these developmental steps in children's play can be dispensed with, and none can be neglected or cut short. All are of inestimable value as foundations for adult life.

The following examples describe a few scenes from the daily life of a Waldorf kindergarten, and show how qualities identified in resilience research (stamina, self-assurance and physical, psychological and mental/spiritual mobility) can be nurtured, along with those key to the salutogenesis approach (comprehensibility, manageability and meaningfulness).

Comprehensibility: grinding corn, baking rolls, communal meal – how children learn to understand the world

A Waldorf kindergarten teacher visits a farm with her kindergarten group. There they first greet the cows in the barn, absorb the warm atmosphere, stroke the cows and watch them eating and chewing the cud. After this they go to the grain barn with its grain sacks: they are all allowed to put their hands in and feel the corn. The group purchases a small amount of grain and takes it back to kindergarten. The next day it is ground up into flour with a hand mill, every child taking a turn in this hard work. The following day a dough is made from the flour, and the children set to work to form whatever their imagination suggests – rolls, balls, worm shapes and many others – which are placed carefully on a baking tray. The trays are put in the oven and baking smells spread through the whole kindergarten. Then everyone sits down at a beautifully laid table. Grace is said or a song is sung, thanking the sun, the rain, Mother Earth or God who made everything grow. Then follows a happy shared meal, after which the day continues.

This small example shows how children gain a little more understanding of the world through these processes, which unfold in five stages of learning and engagement:

- The level of activity: the children were actively and intensively involved; they were 'working'.
- The social level: they accomplished it all together, ate together etc.
- The conceptual level: nothing at all was 'explained' to them, but the children experienced at first hand the logic of the purposeful sequence of different actions.
- The feeling level: the visit to the cows, the smell of the baking rolls, the beautifully laid table.
- The ethical and moral level: the children offered thanks, said grace, sang a song, and in so doing experienced a sense of reverence for creation.

For pre-school children to come to understand the world step by step in a healthy way, their learning and experiences should repeatedly occur at all five of these levels. None of these aspects should be missing, nor should any predominate and squeeze out another. Naturally the example above could be extended with a visit in spring to fields where grain is growing, and in autumn when the corn is cut and threshed. The process of coming to understand the world has no limits. Thus in high school, for instance, Waldorf pupils not only learn how to use a computer but also build simple hardware and software themselves, to gain insight into the way it functions.

Manageability: how self-confidence develops

Children are innately active, and so pre-school Waldorf education is primarily a pedagogy of activity rather than an abstract 'elucidating' pedagogy. This is why life in a Waldorf kindergarten involves a wealth of potential activities.

In the morning, children enter their room and find the teacher sewing something, mending a toy or getting a shared meal ready with a group of children. Other children are playing with a range of simple, natural materials: dolls, boards, cloths, pinecones, ropes, stones etc. Some children organise themselves without help within the mixed age group, while others need an adult's help.

The course of the day is structured: daily circle games reflect the changing seasons, giving expression to diverse characteristics of plants and animals through verses, songs and action sequences (see the essay by J. Walter Baumgartner); meaningful stories with clear progression are repeated on several occasions. Children who experience continual repetitions in a story, a festival, daily routine and so on, gain inner stability.

If young children are given the opportunity to do things themselves, and if their day, week and year become comprehensible to them and structured, their confidence in their own growing abilities will increase. Children will start to feel that they can do things and that they know where they stand, and this gives rise to healthy self-confidence and self-assurance.

But for this developmental process to unfold fully, children must be able to repeatedly look to adults for guidance. Children learn through their own impulses, but imitate adults as they do so. Young children are deeply convinced that the way adults behave is right and good. They enter the world unprejudiced, inquisitive and open, but they can feel lost without the example of adult carers. Rudolf Steiner states the following:

> We have to conceive our physical surroundings in the broadest imaginable scope. They include not only what surrounds children in material terms but everything their senses can perceive occurring in the world around them – what can act upon their spiritual powers from the physical domain. This includes all moral or immoral, all prudent or inept actions that they see.[16]

Meaningfulness

Children observe very precisely how adults do things. Are our actions meaningful or unloving, superficial or engaged? Do our words and actions accord with each other or not? Children perceive our basic psychological and spiritual traits through the way we live, speak and act.

Alongside discovering and nurturing the individual gifts and capacities of each child, the process of education and learning therefore also includes conveying fundamental ethical, moral and religious orientations and values. This is *not* achieved through moralising sermons but through the child's direct perception of the adult's inner stance. This educational process can only properly develop if educating adults repeatedly seek this inner meaning, purpose and orientation in life.

Children aren't looking for perfect carers, but for people making an effort to be inwardly truthful and clear. This prepares them to later discover meaning in their own lives.

In summary we can say that the three basic elements of salutogenesis research – comprehensibility, manageability and meaningfulness – are an inherent constituent of Waldorf education. Research findings from this discipline confirm the value of pedagogical measures in Waldorf schools and kindergartens.

Play means learning – the basic competencies

Children always learn, doing so from the moment they are born. After only a few hours, with the aid of their sense of smell, they form a social bond with their mother; after a few days their sense of hearing supports this relationship between mother and child. As learning beings, from the very outset children use their senses to build up a vital network of social relationships. In the course of their further development, this process becomes increasingly differentiated, and we remain lifelong learners.

For pre-school children, 'implicit' learning is most appropriate. This refers to a mode of learning that takes its lead primarily from tangible examples (model and imitation). Thus young children practise fine motor coordination of their fingers not through specific exercises designed for this purpose, but through the tangible, meaningful actions of daily life, such as baking, crochet and finger-knitting, circle games and finger games.

At school, 'explicit' learning becomes increasingly important. Here children are directed within specific learning situations in a guided, intentional way: numeracy, literacy etc. There are clear divisions between lessons and directed tasks or assignments, a teacher who gives lessons and a single age group. The distinct contents of teaching and learning are presented to children in isolation from other subjects. (It should be mentioned in passing, however, that Waldorf pedagogy counteracts this process of fragmentation with its own unifying methodology and approach to teaching.)

It is often thought that children just play in kindergarten, and only start learning when they go to school. This is a mistaken view and we should try to correct it. Kindergarten children learn intensively, but in a different way from school children. Many education policy makers have this erroneous idea, and try to 'push back' school-based educational content and methods to pre-school age. The Waldorf kindergarten movement continues to oppose this child-endangering outlook with all means at its disposal, and has found allies and partners in the field of neurobiological research.

Before they are ready for school, children learn fundamental capacities, the basic skills on which subsequent schooling can develop. But the decisive difference compared to schooling is this: all children's basic needs, which develop gradually into fundamental capacities, are not imposed from without but are rooted in their own nature. How and when this learning develops is something children themselves determine. It is self-evident that this autonomous developmental process cannot be subject to any kind of assessment or grading.

Basic neurobiological research findings are important in this context. A leading neurobiologist, Gerald Huether, has drawn attention to two fundamental needs and expectations of all children:

1. The need for attachment, connection, protection and security, which children learn in the womb and which is deeply rooted in their brains.
2. The need to learn new things, and pursue tasks that can enable them to grow, such as the need to develop potential, autonomy and freedom. This is why children are so open, so eager to discover things and be creative.

Huether concludes that he is in fact speaking of love as the ideal and developmentally essential human relational form. If loving and secure relationships are lacking between parents, educators and children, the latter will suffer severe physical, emotional, mental and spiritual harm, and the world in general will become more aggressive, adversarial and cold.[17]

Bodily and movement skills

In recent years, scientists, physicians and teachers have observed an ever-increasing number of children with postural deformities, obesity or balance impairment. These children do no get enough physical activity, and their gross and fine motor skills are insufficiently developed. As our psycho-spiritual state corresponds with our physical mobility, if we are unable to balance physically, we are also less likely to be psychologically balanced. Our capacity to move ably and purposefully will also decisively affect speech acquisition. To understand something and engage with it in turn enhances children's capacity to perceive, expands their experiential horizons, and activates the speech development process.

Special attention is therefore given in Waldorf kindergartens to a wide range of movement. Regular walks, games and garden work are just as much part of this range of activity as circle and finger games, craft activities, painting and modelling.

Children who learn to move actively in a wide range of ways are also preparing the ground for increasingly refined capacities of speech and thinking.

Sensory and perceptual competency

Children need to be alert to what's around them and what happens to them. This develops through growing trust in their perceptual powers. For this reason children need reliable, unadulterated sensory impressions in the pre-school years. In Waldorf kindergartens, they experience the real world in a way that is qualitatively shaped and mediated by adults. They use their senses to perceive connections and contexts, thus coming to understand them. Coupling this with their joy at new discoveries, they also gradually experience the primary laws of nature.

Care of the twelve human senses (see p.31) is a major part of pedagogical work. Healthy, naturally-produced food and the use of natural play materials speak authentically to the senses and promote healthy development, as do harmoniously designed spaces, colours and materials.

Media competency, which is needed at a later stage, also requires appropriate pedagogical foundations. To really understand the world, children need to interact with it directly in childhood. Manfred Spitzer writes:

> Only by trying to touch water can I learn what its wetness means. At the same time I hear it gurgle or drip, see its waves or currents, perhaps smell the sea or the grass by the riverbank, and thus gain an overall impression which – together with other such experiences – develops within me into a complex and differentiated representation of water[...]. Thus reciprocal interaction with actual reality is the basis for even starting to engage with the computer's virtual reality. This is why there is no place whatever for computers in a pre-school child's room, kindergarten or nursery.[18]

Virtual worlds deceive us with qualities they do not actually possess. For children to find orientation in virtual reality, they need to be able to rely on their own grounded and well-developed senses first.

Language competency

Thinking and speaking are connected. Only through speech can we express our thoughts, give a name to everything in the world and converse with each other. Children only learn to speak if they grow up in a speech environment. The speech-borne warmth of soul between child and adult provides the soil in which a good, differentiated mode of speaking grows.

In many of the world's countries over the past twenty years, the percentage of pre-school children with speech impediments or speech delay has increased rapidly. In 2002, a study carried out by the Clinic for Communication Disorders at Mainz University found that twenty per cent of three to four-year-old kindergarten children have delayed speech development, and half of these cases are severe enough to require urgent treatment. An additional alarm factor is that no medical causes for these developmental delays were found. Professor Heinemann, director of the study, believes that the causes relate to impoverished speech in families and that too few books are read to children or stories told.[19] The idea of the 'silent family' is currently circulating amongst professionals.

When children learn to relate or narrate things from their own point of view, they are shaping the world according to their impressions. Here also, however, lies the root of problems triggered by premature dominance of modern screen media. Neurobiologists such as Manfred Spitzer and Gerald Huether describe the risk of 'mental debilitation' if children's brains are flooded with alien images at the stage of development when they ought to be learning to develop their own versions of stories and creating their own images.

Rudolf Steiner drew frequent attention to the direct connection between the quality of perceptions and child brain development: 'If the child sees only inept actions before the age of seven, the brain will assume forms that in later life, too, render it fit only for ineptitudes.'[20]

The age at which children start to speak varies individually, but all need good speech models in order to grow into language.

In Waldorf kindergartens, therefore, songs, stories, fairy tales, verses, finger games and circle games are highly valued. Adult carers try to speak in a loving, clear, well-articulated, pictorial and age-appropriate way. So-called 'baby talk' has no place here, and nor do abstract explanations.

Early, active and careful nurturing of speech, and the freedom to express everything without being corrected, along with adults taking time to listen, all provide the basis for the subsequent enjoyment of and skill in reading and comprehension.

Imagination and creativity competency

In our increasingly standardised, pre-packaged and predefined world, being imaginative and creative poses a challenge to education.

Children are innately creative and imaginative. They wish to explore and develop these abilities in kindergarten but they also need the right opportunities to do so. You might hear the following conversation from four and five-year-olds in kindergarten: 'I'll be the mother and you're going to work because you have to earn money. You're the baby and you can be the dog. I'm going to make dinner; it's pizza today. I'm going to build a pizza-flattening machine...'

Children's imaginations incorporate elements of the world they observe and experience: they reshape the world, slip easily into roles and invent wonderful machines. The German psychologist William Stern speaks of 'the child's creative power', based on perceptions and actual experiences on the one hand, but on the other, having its own 'intrinsic power' that enables children 'to create the world in a way that does not actually currently exist'.[21] Human development, both social and cultural, is inconceivable without creativity and imagination.

In Waldorf kindergartens, therefore, development and care of children's imaginations assumes tangible form. Instead of mono-functional, industrially-produced toys, all materials in children's surroundings can be used creatively in play. In role-play and imaginative games every piece of furniture can be used. Stories stimulate them to transform narratives into creative playful activity. Puppet plays presented by the teacher likewise stimulate their imagination and encourage them to create their own puppet shows.

Children's imaginations grasp hold of everything offered, and since children do not yet distinguish between good and bad, it is our pedagogical task to do this for them at this age.

Everything imbued with imagination and artistry broadens and extends our psyche and awareness. Competency in imagination and creativity nurtured in early childhood will help adolescents and adults to develop a wealth of ideas, mental and spiritual mobility, and imagination in the way they shape their lives and work.

Social competency

Children are inherently social from birth and seek to live their way into human interactions and relationships. These learning processes are rooted in the family and continue in kindergarten. In fact, kindergartens today must, more than ever, create foundations for social experience, since there is not always sufficient scope for practising social abilities in some modern family arrangements.

We need communities that can recognise the concerns of each individual, where people can rely on agreements – where rules are followed and trust can thrive. Children specifically need communities where they can learn as many of these social rules as possible and orientate themselves accordingly.

In Waldorf kindergartens, embedded in a sustaining daily and weekly rhythm, children learn that there are rules and individual tasks for each child in the group, such as tidying up, laying the table and watering the flowers. In these activities they can repeatedly observe and imitate adults, learning to take on responsibility. They also witness parents actively helping and participating in the kindergarten community, for instance, renovating its premises or gardening. When toys need to be mended, laundry washed and festivals celebrated together, the children experience a social community that involves and relies on many active people.

For adults, the following meditative thought from Rudolf Steiner can be helpful: 'Health and wholesomeness only come when, in the mirror of the human soul, a reflection of the whole community forms, and in the community lives each soul's separate power.'[22]

Without social competency, an individual's community life is full of conflict and often destructive. If social rules are learned early, effective communities grow, in which everyone can participate, contributing their own interests and skills.

Motivation and concentration

Educational professionals and paediatricians have been discussing the issue of hyperactivity for years. Such children are either diagnosed with attention deficit hyperactivity disorder (ADHD) or generally just find it hard to concentrate. They appear nervous and suffer from sleep disorders and suchlike. Their creative pleasure is hindered and they are unable to focus on particular tasks for any length of time.

Increasingly, such children of kindergarten and school age are now being treated with drugs that 'calm them'. This really only treats the symptoms, not the causes, not to speak of the delayed side effects, which often only become apparent decades later.

Kindergarten work in general cannot extend to medical treatment of severely disturbed children, but it certainly can act preventively, especially since many of these early disorders result from our modern lifestyle: from time pressures, stress, achievement pressures, noise, media exposure and so on. In Waldorf kindergartens, therefore, teachers cultivate a happy, stress-free atmosphere in which children can feel good. Health can thrive in such surroundings.

More than ever today, children need plenty of opportunities to experience coherent sequences of activity and to participate in these actively themselves. By their very nature, young children are interested in lots of things, are inquisitive, and can quickly and easily be diverted or distracted. It is therefore very important that a general sense of stress and rush, of superficiality or boredom, does not pervade the kindergarten. Regular repetition and rhythmic elements in the course of the day, through to an experience of the year and its seasonal cycle, including many special moments and festivals, help to strengthen children's capacity to focus and concentrate.

Children like doing things themselves, and we therefore need to meet this basic need wherever possible and useful. In doing so, though, it is important to remember that offering lots of different input motivates activity far less than the reverse: less is more. Electronic media are completely surplus to requirements in Waldorf kindergartens; not because they are opposed to technology, as such, but because they seek to protect children from injurious influences that work right into brain formation.

Ethical and moral competency

To shape their lives, children and adults need psychological and spiritual orientation, values and tasks to engage with. Children need rules, routine, clarity and truthfulness. This is not about preaching to them. Preaching to children will at most teach them how to preach, but not morality itself.

Here the relation between example and imitation, as set out by Rudolf Steiner, plays a special role:

> Children will be engaged neither by moral exhortations nor rational instructions but by what adults actually *do* visibly in their presence[...]. Healthy vision develops when the child's surroundings are pervaded by the right interplay of light and

> colour, and likewise the physical predisposition for a healthy sense of morality will develop in brain and circulation if children witnesses morality in their surroundings.[23]

Children want to experience adults' loving relationship with nature and perceive their gratitude, for instance in saying grace, and be guided by adults who show care and concern for the elderly, sick people or those in need, and who try to shape social dynamics in a more loving, less adversarial or envious way. Children need parents and teachers who are committed in all kinds of ways – in the kindergarten community, in clubs and associations, in politics.

Children who witness adults repeatedly trying to be clear and truthful, and following high moral standards, will find it easier as adolescents and adults to enhance human dignity in the world.

Noise in kindergarten

The noise levels to which our children are exposed in early years childcare centres is a topic that has come increasingly to the fore in recent years. In Germany, kindergartens have become less protected and enclosed through the introduction of open groups and 'open settings' (which include alternating teachers and the conversion of group rooms into 'open function spaces').

This problem of noise has largely been ignored or sidelined in Germany. Yet background noise and, generally speaking, the framework within which childcare centres operate can have a noticeable impact on children's health and well-being.

Recently, for example, an unusual cry for help from a municipality in Bavaria reached experts in environmental technology at Landshut College of technology. Teachers, children and parents were regularly complaining about the noise levels in local childcare centres, and asking whether this could be reduced.

Using calibrated precision instruments, the noise levels were then measured in a range of settings: council-run, faith-based,

Montessori and Waldorf kindergartens. Measurements were recorded for fifteen minutes in three different situations typical of daily life in childcare: during indoor games, meal times and free play. In council nurseries, the sound level remained almost continuously between 87.8 and 92.7 decibels, equal to the noise of a pneumatic drill at a distance of seven metres. But there was a huge difference between noise levels in council nurseries and Montessori or Waldorf kindergartens! The average physical noise intensity produced by children in the Montessori Children's House was only thirteen per cent, and the Waldorf kindergarten only six per cent, of that in state nurseries. Subjectively, noise levels in the Montessori schools were experienced as being only 54 per cent of that in state nurseries, and in Waldorf kindergartens only 43 per cent.

So far these are only initial measurements. A more extensive study in diverse kindergartens in other cities would be needed to confirm these findings objectively. However, the trend is clear.

The Waldorf method: not hushing children up

Children come into kindergarten in the morning in dribs and drabs. The teacher is busy doing some kind of work: some children join her while others start to play in the doll corner. Others watch for a while. The older children often arrive with fully-fledged ideas and start building a ship or a rocket, using lots of materials and taking up plenty of space. A quarrel may start, but this usually sorts itself out or is settled by the teacher – sometimes simply by suggesting new ideas for play.

In this first free play period of the day, children are welcomed into a structured, pleasant atmosphere that offers plenty of options. Some take their lead from whatever the teacher is doing, while others organise their play themselves, guided by their own imagination or ideas. But they are active. Waldorf education is a pedagogy of activity.

During this period noise levels fluctuate, from very peaceful to loud and boisterous and then calmer again. It all more or less happens by itself as long as children can enter fully into their play activity, and boredom does not rear its head.

Shared break-time

If at all possible, the teacher prepares the break-time snack with a few of the children. Almost all Waldorf kindergartens now have a modern kitchen for this. After a shared song or a verse, the meal can begin. In some kindergartens the children chatter together while they eat; in others they eat quietly for the first few minutes and then, out of this quiet mood, they start to talk. However this happens, the point is for children to experience some moments of quiet and peace during the day, when rush, noise and restlessness are not appropriate. Afterwards busy activity and increasing noise levels resume as the children head for the garden or get ready for a walk. Thus they experience polarities of loud and quiet, and it becomes habitual for them to alternate between these. In an age where permanent background noise predominates, calm and stillness have to be intentionally developed and cultivated.

Children who experience ongoing rhythm and repetition in their lives suffer less from stress and inner restlessness. By learning not only to endure but also to enjoy moments of quiet, followed by the resumption of a joyful racket and boisterous activity, children will be a good deal healthier than those who are driven by inner restlessness.

Ring games and fairy tales

The songs and verses of a ring game often relate to the seasons or narrate an encounter with animals or characters in nature. The accompanying actions often alternate between slow and fast movements, between stretching up high and crouching down low, crawling and running, listening quietly and joyful stamping or clapping: in general between loud and soft.

Kindergarten age is the age for folk and fairy tales. Usually at the end of a busy morning, once children have run about to their hearts' content during the second free play period, it's time to gather in the group room again and listen to a fairy tale or watch a little puppet show.

Peace and quiet is necessary for creating a homely fairy tale mood. As children listen, they let their imaginations waft them away to a fantasy realm, experiencing, for example, the adventures of the initially inept third son who, by the end, overcomes all dangers, marries the princess and wins half the kingdom. Children love these stories, and immerse themselves in their enveloping atmosphere. But increasing numbers of children are so swamped and pervaded by sensory impressions that they find it almost impossible to embrace these brief moments of peace and quiet.

Getting away from the spiral of noise

We cannot protect our children from all sources of noise, but we can be aware that permanent noise is injurious, and seek to balance this in some of the ways described. If not, the noise spiral will go on rising. Such trends can be reversed to ensure kindergartens remain places where young children can develop healthily.

II

Insights into Child Development

The Metamorphosis of Growth Forces into Thinking Forces

Claudia McKeen

Observations of child development from helpless newborn to school age can look in two directions.

In terms of bodily growth, we see children growing bigger, changing in shape and appearance. At the same time their organs and organ functions develop and mature, while sensory perceptions and brain function are elaborated to become ever more complex and interlinked. Children learn to stand upright and walk, speech organs become a tool for speech, while movement capacities increase and become differentiated.

In terms of changes in the psyche: new capacities continually emerge in children's consciousness and their interplay with the world; we can see this, for instance, in the way they play, in speech development, in their ever-more conscious thinking and the development of memory.

These two directions apparently show us two parallel processes of development and maturation: of the physical body and physiology on the one hand, and of the psyche on the other. They are different in each child but nevertheless unfold in accordance with set laws. How are these two processes of development related? Rudolf Steiner answers this question through a primary research finding that he formulates as follows:

> It is of the very greatest importance to know that our ordinary powers of thinking are refined powers of form and growth. A spiritual element manifests in the way the human organism grows and assumes shape; and this spiritual force subsequently appears in the course of life as our powers of thinking.[24]

This means that the body's life forces and powers of regeneration, which enable children to grow and develop their organs and remain active in adult organ function and regeneration, are the same as those we use to think, to form our ideas and to remember.

In fact, we have first-hand experience of this connection between the powers of the psyche and those at work in the body's physiological processes. We grow warm when we experience something beautiful, or feel palpitations when something alarms us, or blush when we're ashamed. In the fields of psycho-immunology and salutogenesis, too, a wide range of scientific studies confirms these connections. It has been shown in laboratory tests, for instance, that negative thoughts and feelings, despondency and despair, experiences of loss and depression, demonstrably reduce our blood's immune defences. On the other hand, positive thoughts and feelings, such as enthusiasm, hope, tranquillity and joy have a stimulating effect on our physiological immune system.

This dual aspect of life forces, responsible on the one hand for growth, regeneration, healing and reproduction, and on the other acting as bearer of conscious thinking and memory, is of fundamental importance for education. In this view, education is no longer just tasked with conveying knowledge and culture, but must also bear responsibility for bodily health. At every moment, as educators, we have to be aware that in accompanying children's growth and development we are drawing on the forces available for learning, and that all cognitive learning also affects physical health throughout a person's life.

This insight follows from the anthroposophic view of the human being and underpins Waldorf education. It leads to a concept of development that is radically different from the traditional one, and therefore looks for a completely different educational methodology. Here it is no longer primarily a matter of conveying knowledge or information but of adapting learning steps to what is currently happening in bodily development: to the forces of growth released from the body that become free for specific activities of heart and mind.

Modern educational discourse presumes that young children basically have the same structures of thought and feeling, the same intellectual parameters and capacities of awareness as adults, though in a more limited, imperfect form. In this view, development, educational support and learning involve enhancing these intellectual capacities in a linear, ascending process of accumulating knowledge. The inevitable consequence of this idea is anxiety on the part of many parents and teachers that children might miss out on something if they do not learn as soon as possible what they are meant to know later on.

The anthroposophic view, by contrast, does not see child development in linear terms but in phases and metamorphoses. The life forces that were initially active in shaping and forming the body appear in a following phase as powers of awareness in the psyche. Here it is not a matter of teaching children a great deal as early as possible, devising programmes of learning to explain to them how the world works, nor expecting that they will retain all this in their memory. On the contrary, education focuses instead on strengthening the powers of growth, the life forces, enabling children to grow healthily and become physically skilful. To do so children need to experience the world through all their senses as it really is, to *grasp* things bodily and unconsciously that they only later come to understand consciously. What children experience in their bodies thus becomes the foundation for subsequent intellectual faculties.

In nature, we find linear developmental laws in the mineral realm. A crystal, whether big or microscopically small, always follows the physical and chemical laws inherent in it. It invariably grows through the external depositing and accumulation of substance, and every change involves a purely quantitative addition or subtraction of substance, implicit in the laws of substance. No transformation occurs. In every living creature, on the other hand, metamorphosis is the inherent law of development. In other words, phases subject to very different laws build upon each other. Each phase requires its own conditions and time to form the foundation for the next stage of development. This is true particularly in children. The more time a phase is allowed to come to full fruition, the sounder and more perfectly developed subsequent phases will be.

During foetal development the forces of growth and configuration are most strongly focused on the body; and in the early years, too, they are still intensively absorbed in growth and maturation of organ forms and functions. As organs and functions mature, we see children's awareness wake up. The head with the nervous system and sense organs is most developed at birth, and this is the sphere in which children first awaken to their surroundings. This alertness of the senses is connected with imitation – the developmental gateway through which, still entirely unconsciously, children in the first three years learn to walk, speak and think by feeling, experiencing and embodying what they perceive in their surroundings. By this means they further develop their body and organs and gain physical agility and skill. At this age, therefore, we speak of children's 'sensorimotor intelligence', although this involves not only the motor system but is a form of intelligence bound to the body and active within it.

Between the ages of three and five, children's breathing and circulation systems primarily mature and settle into their individual rhythm. At this stage children's speech organs also form, and they learn to say complex sounds, sound combinations and sentences. In the psyche, imagination unfolds. Children imitate processes in the world around them, especially the activities of adults, and inwardly transform all they experience by ensouling objects and attributing the most diverse meanings to them. Everything comes alive as living beings that speak to children, telling them about the world and seeking to be known by them.

At five and six the first major morphological change occurs – a transformation of the child's whole shape, demonstrating readiness for school. The body extends and becomes more clearly formed: neck, waist and joints become more pronounced and the chest flattens. In particular, the limbs extend and assume clearer shape. Agile, harmonious movements are also typical of this age, as is the beginning of second dentition, when milk teeth are replaced by permanent teeth. New capacities for learning and thinking develop, in particular the ability to recall memories independently.

If, in the first five to six years, children meet the world through many conceptual, abstract explanations instead of directly, unconsciously experiencing it, their developmental forces will be prematurely channelled into thinking and memory functions, thus being withdrawn from their formative work on the body and its organs. In such cases imitation often wanes, children tend to look pale, and to be restless and nervous. The danger of incomplete or poor bodily maturation arises. The health consequences of this, though, usually only become apparent in later years.

Child development in these early years, therefore, requires education to support formative growth forces in their work on the body. Taking account of this reality means providing a foundation for health. If we allow children time to build up their body and structure their organs, so that growth forces are fully able to develop their sensorimotor capacities, they will later grasp and understand more thoroughly what they have first accomplished bodily.

As adults we have all experienced the connection between organ-forming life forces and conceptual thinking and memory, for example during a feverish illness that leaves us fully preoccupied with our body. In such circumstances we have no desire to be mentally active and it seems very hard indeed to follow a complex sequence of ideas. Instead, to recover, we seek peace, withdrawal and release from daily tasks and problems. The forces of growth and regeneration plunge back into and involve themselves in the body. Once we have recovered, we feel that we can take up our conscious role in life again with renewed strength.

Rudolf Steiner coined the terms 'life forces', 'formative forces' and also 'etheric forces' for these powers, which, though not apparent to sensory perception, take visible effect. They are an interconnected, mutually-coordinated system of forces penetrating the whole body. What invisibly imbues and shapes the physical body is therefore also called 'life body' or 'ether body'.

A few examples below aim to show the way bodily, form-developing powers achieve this transition into forces of awareness, and into the creation and shaping of mental images.

Powers facilitating standing and movement, and our inner relationship to space

Being born means leaving the weightlessness and protection of the mother's body and entering the outside world. One of the most incisive experiences here must surely be that of gravity. During pregnancy the child floated in the amniotic fluid, lived in weightlessness and uplift. The newborn child becomes fully subject to the sway of earth's gravity. Learning to stand and walk means overcoming gravity. In engaging and coming to terms with gravity and lightness, achieving a vertical stance and an initially unsteady balance in standing and walking, children learn to establish their own relationship with space. By doing so they reconfigure their bodies into an upright form. This affects and reshapes all their organs and limbs. Even their bones, through the finest structures, the trabeculae, are altered by this interplay of weight and lightness.

The experience of these inner self-raising powers becomes apparent in play when, from about fifteen months, children, with great concentration, start building towers by placing bricks on top of each other. Some well-intentioned adults try to show children that it is easier to make first a foundation of horizontal bricks. This is based, though, on a misunderstanding of what's happening here. Children want to build using vertical, upward-directed forces that are released from the body. Only six months later – usually around 21 months – comes the next phase of placing bricks in horizontal rows. By then children have learned to walk, to actively conquer surrounding space. From around thirty months children achieve the balance and security of movement in three-dimensional space required to build spatial forms such as steps, which are simultaneously horizontal and vertical. It becomes clear how children initially work with bodily forces, which subsequently become their own outward activity, and eventually develop further into conscious understanding of the world.

What children first form bodily and then practise in play as unconscious experience awakens in a further stage as understanding of speech, and can then be properly applied as concepts. This becomes evident by observing the sequence of phases in young children's play in relation to language. Brick constructions are preceded from around six months by a stage of play referred to as 'container play', involving filling and emptying containers. Then follows the phase we have described of vertical, then horizontal and finally three-dimensional building (see Figure 1); then speech development and conscious understanding. First children can understand the word 'in' and a little later use this correctly; then follows understanding and use of 'on'; somewhat later comes 'beside'; and, for concepts relating to three-dimensional space, 'under' and 'behind'.

For education this means that as long as children are in the container play phase, we should not offer them tower and row building, or encourage this, but instead give them the opportunity to practise as much filling and emptying as they wish. Generally, the better each developmental stage is practised and can mature, the more stably anchored bodily strength will be, and consequently the better and more securely it can be transformed into other skills.

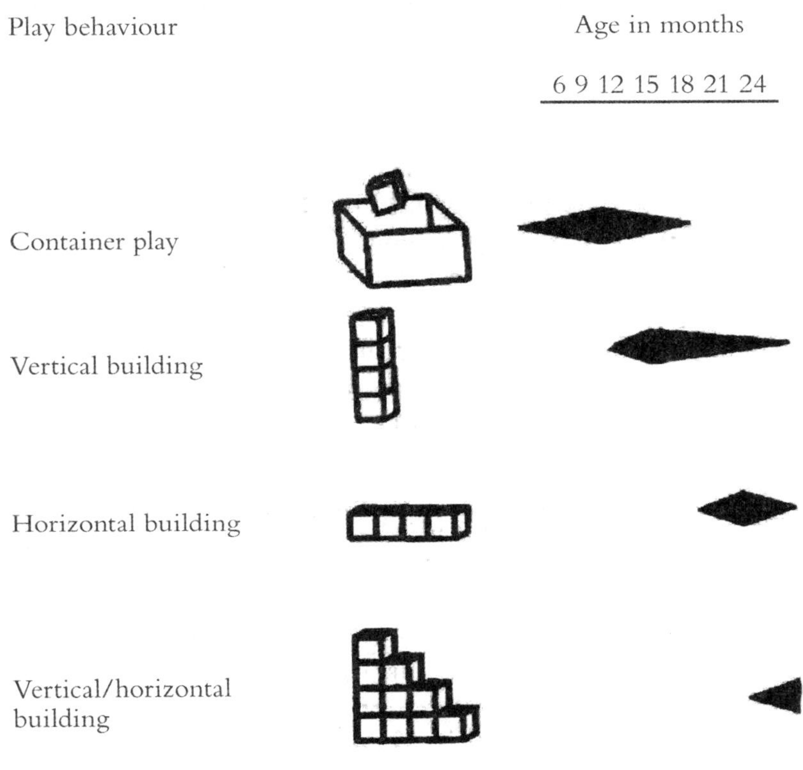

Figure 1. Play phases [25]

From the body's formative forces to a conscious grasp of forms

We can observe how the forces active in the body surface in awareness through children's relationship to space and to the shapes in their surroundings. By learning to stand upright and move through space, children gain an unconscious, bodily experience of vertical and horizontal. But as yet they have no awareness of dimensions and spatial forms, cannot conceive them and inwardly picture them. Young children cannot yet estimate distances, and, for example, happily look at picture books upside down.

Not until the age of seven or eight does children's awareness free itself from unconscious bodily experience to become conceptual experience. At this stage children develop a new relationship to their body: they become conscious of their own form, and their body image is consolidated. They can now move limbs separately from each other, so that the right or left hand can perform movements without the other side joining in – indispensable, not least for learning to write. Laterality develops, and they can increasingly distinguish right from left. They become aware of forward and backward dimensions. The bodily experiences accumulated in the first five to six years, and incorporated into the body, become free as concepts and make inner mental picturing possible. They can compare one shape with another, notice that something is missing from otherwise identical shapes, and copy more complex shapes with changes of direction.

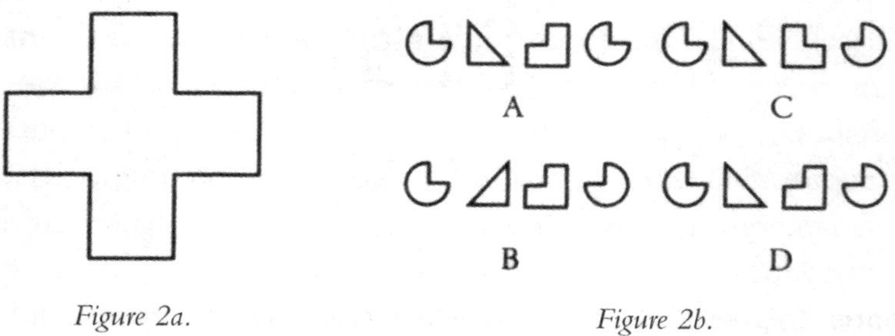

Figure 2a. *Figure 2b.*

Figure 2a. Shape with change of direction. To copy the cross, children must look at the drawing and inwardly retain the image they see after looking away, then transfer their inner image onto a piece of paper.

Figure 2b. Shapes with different spatial orientations. Here children must recognise the same shape under different, but similar conditions, and in a range of spatial positions. This requires spatial perception and the capacity to retain what they see in their awareness and compare it.

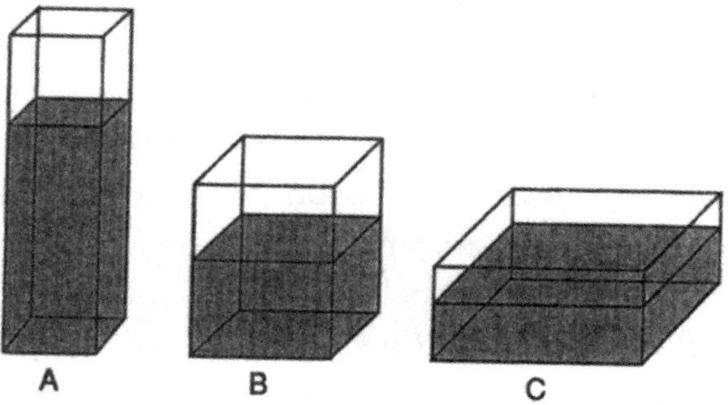

Figure 3. Constant quantities and volumes. The three containers hold the same amount of liquid. Children of pre-school age say that container A has most liquid because the level is highest.[26]

Children can also now judge constant forms accurately, even when they appear in different positions (so-called visuomotor coordination and the ability to recognise inner coherence of form. See Figure 2b). All this depends on the capacity to move within an inwardly conceived space, requiring a conscious inner grasp and picturing of form that is retained when the gaze is turned away from one form to another, or when a shape seen only in the mind's eye is copied onto paper. Children must retain a shape in their minds in order to detect the difference between one and the other. When we do geometry at a later stage we draw on these powers, accomplishing in pure thinking the movements we carried out physically as young children.

Understanding of spatial dimensions and the constancy of quantities and volumes is something children only acquire at primary school age (see Figure 3). Practical experience is the basis for subsequent insight into the relationship between the shape of a container and its contents. Only by repeatedly pouring the same contents into different containers can children understand this relationship, and this learning process cannot be cut short by explanations and instruction.

Bodily foundations for remembering and thinking in images

The capacity to remember experiences, and to actively call forth images of past events without this being triggered by a present experience, usually arises between the ages of five and six. Reproducing experiences requires a power of retention that can fix them in clear, distinct and enduring contours, without sequences of events becoming confused or forgotten. This new skill occurs at around the same time as permanent teeth complete their development.

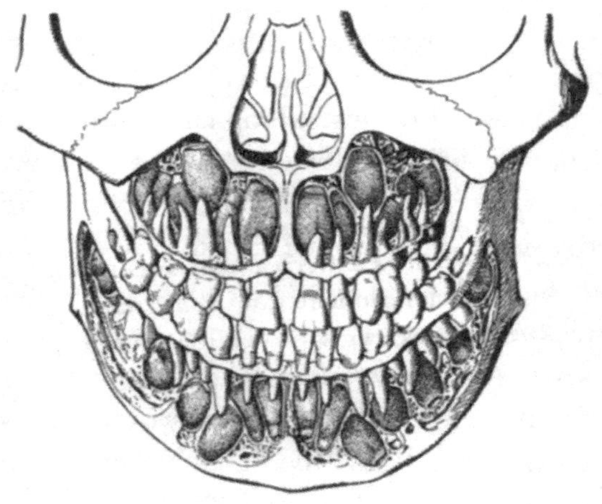

Figure 4. Milk teeth with permanent teeth waiting to come through in the jaw of a six-year-old child.

Below the full set of twenty milk teeth, the 32 permanent teeth (twenty to replace the milk teeth and twelve new molars, not including the wisdom teeth) are already formed and wait in the jaw ready to emerge gradually over the next six to seven years. The dentition-forming powers have created organ structures and substance processes characterised by duration, stability and absolute form retention. These are now no longer needed to form teeth. We find them instead metamorphosed in consciousness, as the powers of memory, which give our images and thoughts clear, lasting contours. These enable us to remember the beginning of a story when we have got to the end, and recall, unaltered, things we have retained in our mind.

Before these forces are freed from the body, children's experiences fade from their awareness. Things can then be remembered through an external stimulus. In a five-year-old, pictures and ideas formed when looking at things quickly fade. Peter Rosegger relates an experience he had at the age of five: he started to cry at school, and when the teacher asked him what was wrong he said he'd forgotten what his mummy looked like. He was not yet able to retain ideas and images and recall them at will – though he already knew he'd forgotten something important. We can see the power of memory starting to work when a six-year-old can imagine, without prompting, 'I'm in the sandpit in the garden right now,' and then, shortly afterwards, 'and now I'm with Grandma in the living room,' followed by, 'and now I'm in the mountains where we lost the pocket knife,' and finally, excitedly, 'Can you do that too, imagine you are wherever you like?'

The transition from kindergarten to school

Learning in kindergarten and school are fundamentally different. In kindergarten, learning is implicit: everything comes from direct experience. At school, learning becomes explicit: things and connections in the world are explained to children in a way they need to think about, understand and remember. Learning increasingly occurs through hearing, whereas vision is the primary sense used at kindergarten, through which events in children's surroundings are absorbed directly as images, eliciting an unconscious response or outward action.

We can gauge readiness for school by observing when children have the ability to pass from implicit to explicit learning. This cannot be linked to a fixed date and age but is determined by the individual child's developmental dynamic. It can be identified, on the one hand, by a change in body shape, and on the other, by the new capacities of recall and free picturing that surface in the psyche – a more alert relationship to the world and other people. Specifically at this transitional period, it is very important to pay full attention to these interconnected factors: the dual aspect of growth forces. The sooner children are guided towards targeted thinking and picturing, or asked to remember things, the sooner forces are withdrawn from their bodily organism that they may still need for growing.

The transition from implicit to explicit learning occurs in the last year of kindergarten, when five and six-year-olds start planning their games in advance. When they arrive at kindergarten in the morning they may already know who and what they want to play with, and what materials they will need. Or they may resume yesterday's game and carry on playing it for several successive days. In doing so they clearly announce their new inner powers. These children would no doubt already cope with formal schooling, but then they would miss out on an important experience: doing what they themselves have imagined and decided to do. In the early years, the content of learning – which usually fades and is forgotten – is much less important than what is done. This autonomous activity, when five or six-year-olds turn ideas of their own into play, is something they should be allowed time to practise intensively. By doing so they acquire a capacity that no instruction can provide: self-determined, planned undertakings; shaping and developing their own ideas and memories and realising them in action. These capacities are more valuable in later life than early schooling (such as learning to read) at this age.

The more children's developmental forces can be nurtured in

kindergarten, so they are not drawn prematurely out of unconscious bodily activity through explanations, or by over-stimulation of memory, the better their subsequent schooling can work. The powers of thinking, remembering and understanding that are used for learning in school must be prepared and nurtured in kindergarten by establishing their corporeal foundation. Children need time, since healthy development takes time to bring each phase to full fruition. Then the foundation of health is laid for the whole of a person's life.

Understanding Children's Drawings

Angelika Prange

Observe children drawing between the ages of two and six and you can be astonished at the concentrated, intense, clear and assured way they create circles, lines, patterns and motifs. In Waldorf kindergartens, children can draw during the free play period: this helps them settle or, for instance, make the transition into play or move into a different activity after helping prepare the shared break. Some children come away from playing to draw, immerse themselves in this and then go straight back to playing again.

Drawing is a key and natural activity for children. We collect, name and date the pictures they create over one, two, three and sometimes even four years. When children leave kindergarten we give them these drawings in a fat book as a farewell. If you look at these books you can clearly detect an individual nuance in the sequence of images, but in general what you find is a lawfulness corresponding to the developmental stage and age of the child. In these first seven years, children – passing from helpless infant to self-aware, grounded school children, eager to learn – acquire fundamental and vital skills. From lifting the head, rolling, crawling, sitting up, standing, children move on to walking, running, climbing stairs, hopping, jumping, stilt-walking and rope skipping. Children increasingly bring movement and stillness into harmony within a larger sequence of movements, and coordination of the fine motor skills become ever more differentiated. By rising seven, therefore, children can tie their laces, open and close buttons and slice fruit with a knife. They learn to use scissors to cut paper, sew with a sharp needle and much more.

Language development culminates at this age in grammatically correct sentences and an ever more extensive vocabulary. Children will often know by heart the fairy tales they have been told, and can speak or sing verses, rhymes and a treasury of songs encompassing the whole year. All this arises from imitative play and perception. At the same time a stable kindergarten community allows social and emotional skills to develop.

Parallel to this, children learn to recognise contexts and sequences, passing from developing memory to an incipient capacity for thinking, until new powers of thinking and learning emerge quite clearly when they are ready for school.

We can discern specific stages in these developing capacities, although of course individuals vary a good deal. Children's innate impulse to imitate enables them to shape their inherited body from the head (neurosensory system) through the central chest realm (rhythmic system) to the feet (metabolic and limb system). In the process, the child's individuality endows the ether body (body of formative forces) with impulses of soul and spirit. This process of shaping and configuring lays the physical, constitutional foundations for a person's whole life. Parents and teachers need to accompany this decisive developmental phase of life with much love, care, attentiveness and pleasure but also with alert interest and a skilled eye.

As suggested, the various stages of development can be detected by observing children's movement, speech and thinking, as well as their social and emotional maturity in play. In their outward appearance, too, and the expressive possibilities of their drawings, children show us the current stage of their body-transforming development. The comments below describe patterns that can be found in children's drawings, running parallel to their physical development and the different phases in play up to rising seven.

From birth to rising three children are embedded in a wealth and breadth of sensory impressions. Their power to imitate enables them to gradually take inner hold of their body in continuous practice. Walking is still tentative, often on tiptoes, speech is limited to short phrases, but in thinking we can already see children connecting sensory perceptions into contexts and sequences. Children practise and are tirelessly and creatively active. However, continual care and attention are needed: outer boundaries, warm protection and enclosure in the form of rhythm, good habits, rituals and a meaningful context.

In this way the basal senses are nurtured, especially the senses of life and touch, while the senses of own movement and balance are cultivated by standing and walking. At rising three, children first start to draw: lack of motor control produces 'back and forth' and 'up and down' scribbles, or a circular archetypal spiral pattern. These first scribblings still testify to 'unconscious life': a wealth of outward gestures that children allow to arise as though in passing (Figures 1 and 2). At this stage children are preoccupied with developing the neurosensory system and, through continuous practice and activity, they transmit impulses into the structures of the developing brain.

The archetypal spiral is one of the ever-repeating patterns children express in drawings. In this 'knot' we can sense children's inwardly enclosed existence, giving expression to the brain's structure and showing us the phase of physical development in which children are currently engaged. Out of the mobile dynamic of their whole being they place themselves creatively in the world. Children can spend months drawing circles with alternating pendulum movements in various combinations until, finally, the circle is closed. This occurs with intensity and full involvement of the psyche (Figure 3).

What does the closing of the circle symbolise? Between the ages of two and three, the cranial sutures close. The child's head closes off and at the same time full sensory openness recedes. The child starts to detach and feel separate from the world – a time also when ego or 'I' consciousness emerges. The first phase of defiance and tantrums begins. Children will now often draw closed circles with a will-accentuating point at their centre.

Towards the age of three, children's cosmic awareness transforms into earthly consciousness. Cosmic consciousness surrounding the body withdraws increasingly like a vortex, and earthly awareness concentrates, orienting itself to earthly things. Children master a new home, passing from archetypal spirals and knots, though always still in movement, to a closed circle and point. Now they start to see themselves as autonomous beings: as they grow more individual they delimit themselves as an 'I' with the circle. The point at its centre is saying, 'Here I am' (Figure 4).

Working with the powers of soul and spirit, the life forces have by now created a basic structure in the brain, achieved through repeated, practised activity. Once children have taken full hold of the head realm, infant memory becomes available to them, and they enter a quite new developmental phase. They start to distance themselves from the surrounding world on the one hand, and on the other to absorb it in a new dimension of the psyche. A sense of inner and outer worlds develops. Children increasingly perceive themselves as individuals and demonstrate a new awareness. Three-year-old children now start drawing feeler-like threads that emerge from the closed circle. Head and trunk are, in children's awareness, still merged as one (Figure 5). These drawings are first attempts to depict a human form, a self-image. The closed circle is the starting point for perceiving the surrounding world anew, more consciously, through the feelers of the senses.

Over the next few years, children acquire an individual inner psychological space, perceiving themselves and the outer world in an increasingly complex way. We can see this advance in play, language development, movement, social interactions and in the understanding of meaningful contexts. Play first unfolds in a group of children in parallel creative activity, rather than interaction. Materials are arbitrarily involved, re-organised, lined up together; and in this fluctuating activity another object will soon draw the child's interest. We see this in children's drawings, too, in which everything is as yet a colourful, dynamic chaos of things randomly juxtaposed (Figure 6).

This initial parallelism changes into interaction. Little dens made of wooden stands covered in cloths give the necessary peace and enclosure for older and younger children to play together, and to engage in diverse learning in role-play.

Here the 'big ones' – the five and six-year-olds – take the lead and allocate roles: taking care of the dolls, for instance, going shopping, cooking and baking. The three and four-year-olds are mostly the 'children' while the older ones are the 'grown-ups'. To begin with, the three-year-olds will often run from one house to the next. They may just sit there, looking on in wonder or joining in; or help the adults engaged in some purposeful activity. They feel good in this atmosphere of busy activity. Drawings of the 'head-and-feet' person clearly tell us that children have grasped hold of their bodies. They engage with the world now in an ever more assured way and gradually take firm possession of a solid trunk (Figures 7 and 8).

This 'trunk person' still initially resembles a tree. Children increasingly incorporate their surroundings, grounding their drawings on the earth or grass.

The sky and the sun are introduced, and this extended relationship to the outside world reveals the action of a new realm of powers (Figures 9 and 10). With the step from the 'head-and-feet person' to 'trunk person' (or 'tree person') children show us their new awareness and perceptions. Their imaginative powers awaken, giving rise to rich and diverse play, and a whole new colourful world. Physically, the child's middle realm, the rhythmic system, is forming.

Four-year-olds are now engaging more with each other socially and can take on roles more fully. They perceive their surroundings and themselves more consciously and increasingly find their 'own place' and sense of stability (Figure 11).

In drawings at this stage there are many images of sequenced forms and 'ladders' that create separate chambers within the whole design. At this time the child's vertebral column is stabilising, with the ribcage, lungs, heart and bronchial tubes; outwardly, dominance of this middle realm gives the child a more rounded appearance. We can see the intensity of this bodily maturation in a new rhythmic shaping of human figures and landscape, with 'ladder people', railways tracks and fences appearing as new motifs in drawings (Figures 12 and 13). The spine and vertebrae are consolidating and the ribs are hardening. The skeleton becomes solid, and abdominal breathing now takes over from diaphragm breathing. Tree landscapes look like costal arches (Figure 14). The tree trunks, branches, twigs, leaves and developing crowns represent an image of the lungs and of strengthening respiration. The motif of the square or rectangle, drawn as house and body, testify to a surer, more solid inhabiting of the body (Figure 15). Children now draw bold, colourful, patterned images, such as a spiral around a central point, enclosing this with chambers and wing forms. We see a 'heart spiral' that suggests a living, rhythmic centre (Figures 16 and 17). At this age, children's flourishing, soul power of imagination is taking hold of the world, and shaping it inwardly in ever-greater abundance.

A new quality of soul feeling, of rich experience with materials in their surroundings, and close, meaningful inner connection with significant others, give children a new capacity for equilibrium. Pictures quite clearly showing an axis of symmetry develop: the division of paper into four areas – of a whole pattern or as separate 'windows'. These lively, colourful images demonstrate an order and rhythm in their engagement with space (Figures 18 and 19). Children increasingly live in the wealth of their imaginative pictures. This needs to be supported and sustained, however, by an outer framework of good habits, and a daily, weekly and yearly rhythm. Fairy tales, rhymes, songs and finger games give children a necessary sense of order, and the rhythmic repetition of speech nurtures organ development.

Repeated rhythms give security and self-confidence. Alongside symmetrical pictures, all kinds of patterns now emerge, typical of five-year-olds. These diverse variations seem to arise from an inner need. Children now like drawing together. A new sense of 'we' arises, of the group: they come to the drawing table in twos and threes, and tirelessly invent new patterns (Figure 20).

Children seek order, structure and proportion. The space on the paper is divided into different areas and they try out possible relationships of large/small, bright/dark, pointed/rounded, thick/thin, and so on (Figure 21).

At this age, children engage with the world in an ever more assured way. Their bodily experience becomes more varied. The 'trunk or tree person' has become more grounded. Perceptions now repeatedly orient themselves to intensively experienced regions of the body, as can be seen in Figure 22, where the fingers are the focus of perception. Children still live in 'sensory memory': what they see, smell, hear and taste kindles a light that allows things they have experienced to resurface in their minds.

Children's fine motor skills develop, and their agility and coordination become more assured. They are willing to try walking on stilts, balancing and skipping with a rope in a group. The dens they build in free play time are no longer just for seclusion and protection but involve playful experimentation. They develop a wide range of activities: caring for dolls, organising and furnishing the house, visiting neighbours and shopping. A new, active social aspect broadens the scope of play. Children become 'mobile', both inwardly and outwardly. In their drawings this mobility and skilfulness is expressed in wheels, some with faces, which adorn houses (Figure 23).

The house is a central motif representing physical life and inhabiting of the body. If a house has windows and doors, the child's senses are likely to be alert and attentively observing the world. A smoking chimney testifies to the activity that is taking place in the house: a fire has been lit there, the house is warm and comfortable. The square is the fundamental symbol in this active, imaginative phase of development, whereas the circle predominated in the first two-and-a-half years. The body, the house, the swing – everything is square, telling us that the child has arrived on the earth (we can see this clearly in Figure 15).

Five-year-old children will often withdraw for a while,

sometimes expressing boredom, lack of energy or enthusiasm. This process can be brief or last many weeks. Children draw back from imaginative experiences and from a previously dynamic outpouring of energy: second dentition is approaching, and their powers turn inward for a while in order to develop the very hardest substance of the teeth. In Figure 24 the child has closed the house with a portcullis. The little adjoining tower, which stands to one side, is crowned with jagged points. At this age, anxieties can emerge more strongly. Children are sensitive and can be tearful. They seek understanding attention and acknowledgement, and it can help to join them in activities such as crafts, preparing break-time, tidying, sweeping, and so on.

Once this phase has passed, a new, energetic and above all focused developmental period begins. From rising six, children 'work' within their system of limbs and metabolism. Physical movements during this growth period are initially angular in nature, but towards the age of six become lithe and more differentiated in both gross and fine motor skills. Legs and feet, arms and hands become skilled at rope skipping, throwing and catching a ball, walking on stilts and balancing on a tree trunk. This coordination gives them more freedom. Children come to kindergarten with a new awareness, knowing precisely what they want to play. Certain materials, corners of the room and utensils are chosen quickly and intentionally. They eagerly await the arrival of certain friends. Their memory transforms into an incipient power of thinking.

Connections are recognised, 'functions' invented: for instance a tightrope is stretched across the room, divers' goggles and oxygen cylinders are created from pieces of wood and ribbons, and put on, and the ocean floor is explored for fish and sunken treasure. Children 'stage' things they have experienced: houses, restaurants, sailing boats and hospitals are built. Events are now drawn in a way that relates to reality. In Figure 25, for instance, an annual apple-juice pressing event is depicted.

Children can now articulate their thoughts. They are perceptibly more distanced and conscious in their representation of the world, and thus increasingly self-aware. In Figure 26 the child is inside the house with bowls full of food; the Christmas tree takes pride of place, crowned with a star. The child on the right stands beside a gift, and there is a gift under the other child's chair. In Figure 27 the farmer is going off to the cornfield with his scythe to harvest his crop. A new symbol appears, the triangle, in the expansive and energetic stride of the farmer.

In summary, we can see that in the first two-and-a-half years children acquire the neurosensory foundations of walking, speaking and thinking, and reconfigure this into sensory memory. This gives rise to children's first grasp of awareness of their distinct individuality. Children draw circles, themselves as a circle, and the 'I point'. The head predominates here.

Over the next two years, roughly until their fifth birthday, the middle realm of the rhythmic system is etherically engaged, and the power of imagination develops. Children learn to shape the world in a dreamy way, growing their psyche. They connect with the world, draw themselves as a square and the middle region of the trunk predominates. Now children develop rich imaginative lives, and memory transforms into an incipient power of thinking. In subsequent transformation of the motor and metabolic systems, the will is engaged. The limbs grow longer. Now the powers that were bound to the body become free and available for learning. The triangle is the predominant symbol here, appearing in the house, the human body, and the robes of the Three Kings and their crowns. Dynamic zigzags are expressed frequently in pattern pictures, intimating that second dentition is approaching or has begun (Figures 28 and 29). The girl who drew these two pictures was aged six years, five months, and was still awaiting her second teeth.

In the following pictures a new motif emerges: that of animals. The child riding the horse has a triangular body, and has not yet taken hold of the reins (Figure 30). The animal itself possesses a sleeping consciousness, follows its instincts. In the next developmental step children start engaging and working on the metabolic realm, as the animal does – in a kind of sleeping awareness. This period is sometimes accompanied by stomach aches and boredom. In Figure 31 the horse has now been harnessed to a coach and is being safely guided by the reins. This insecure transitional period has been overcome.

Children engage energetically with the world in jumping, hopping and running. They become skilful, strong and self-confident. This newly acquired agility extends as far as the fingertips and toes. In eurythmy, for instance, children can now run on tiptoe, while imitating the sparkling stars over their heads in fine finger movements. Increasingly conscious and more distanced, they perceive their experiences and respond to their surroundings. They can enact and accompany all this with their bodies, and actively exert their will. This engagement with the world also becomes apparent in ever-clearer thinking and in increasing powers of expression through speech.

Children now grasp whole contexts of meaning and can orient themselves in space and time. They can use their memory to visualise experiences. Individual creativity acquires new forms of expression, which is represented in drawings of scenes.

Up to the age of seven, therefore, children show us their current stage of development in many ways, indicating how their own individuality, with powers of mind and soul, is penetrating and shaping the body they have inherited from their parents, and how they take hold of the physical foundations for their future lives.

Free Play: a Spring of Learning

Marie-Luise Compani

Play is each child's profession!
Achim Kranz

The complex pre-school educational programmes that are being developed in many of the world's countries, or which already exist, are robbing children of their intrinsic and essential need to play. Instead they are being asked to learn, and to reflect on their experiences of this process. A striking number of children in various kinds of pre-school care no longer know how to play. The most natural thing in a child's life is frequently passed over.

The capacity for play develops in earliest childhood, with respective phases of play reflecting children's stages of development. But what is the distinctive nature of children's play?

It is completely non-goal oriented. Children do not play in order to solve some task or other, or for a reward; yet they always invest meaning and purpose in their play – it is never meaningless! When playing they use all forms of physical, sensory experience, pictorial ideas, subjective fantasies, language-based or non-language-based thinking, as well as social interaction and communication. Play shapes all these into a connected process.

When playing, children move in a sphere independent of time and space. Everything is possible in the imagination, yet here too there are clear boundaries. Play unfolds as a temporal sequence with a beginning and an end, with points of culmination and phases of fading interest, of stimulus, excitement, relaxation, absorption or physical action, of being alone or gathering with others. In this way children find their own mode of structuring time, their own rhythm for doing things.

Motivating opportunities that challenge children and invite them to play are a precondition for the capacity to play. Play itself is something they configure themselves. They connect their inner experience with the outer world, and what they experience in doing so in turn informs their inner experience. These impressions are reflected in the neurophysiological processes of children's brains. Through play children gain many complex and sensory experiences, engaging in a productive, creative process in which past experiences are re-thought and re-assembled in repeated experimentation.

In this context the psychotherapist Eckehardt Schiffer speaks of 'intermediary spaces' – openings or interspaces that arise as children play, where they can experience themselves in imaginative activity. This also includes the dialogues that arise in play between two or more people. In self-forgetfulness children enter these intermediary spaces and return from them enriched.

What happens in such spaces is something children initially absorb as implicit knowledge, which is true of all experiences they incorporate through the senses, motor functions and feelings. What they learn through play is stored in explicit, 'declarative' memory, and the more opportunities they have been given to connect their declarative memory with what has occurred in the intermediary spaces of play, the better they can draw on past experience. Children who build a house or den using boards and play stands are engaging playfully and imaginatively with structural laws – otherwise the house would collapse. These play experiences give children implicit understanding which is, however, stored as tangible experience in their declarative memory. They can access what they have experienced, and now know how to build a house that will stand up.

The fundamental mood of children's play is cheerful yet serious. The seriousness with which they go about their play is similar to an adult's attitude to work. But unlike the adult, there are no externally imposed objectives that constrain their play. They play out of their imagination and ideas, trying to bring their inner and outer reality into harmony.

This quite naturally gives rise to pleasure in playing and learning. Motivation lies within and not outside them, which is the reason for the term 'intrinsic motivation'. Children want to learn and know things; they are full of the joys of discovery. The sense of exploring the world and of ordering and perceiving it in meaningful contexts is a key motif for every child from birth onwards.

The meaning of attachment for free play

Besides pleasure and interest, which motivate children to play, attachment and its development are also important. Children want to be accepted, acknowledged and loved. For their mental and socio-emotional development they need confirmation and affirmation from those closest to them. An infant's first smile elicits the parents' greatest joy, initiating a dialogue of smiles between them and their child. Infants then feel accepted, loved and affirmed, and this creates the basis of trust between child and parents. Reliability and a regular daily routine, along with habits and little rituals, meet their need for security and protection.

Being aware of and responding sensitively to a child's needs creates the foundation for secure attachment between child and parents: a safe harbour from which children can set out to explore the world. When danger rears its head, they seek protection and security from their parents, upon whom they know they can rely.

These early experiences of attachment are formative and decisive for later life. Brain research has shown that inadequate or insecure attachment is a poor foundation for childhood development. Where this is the case, children will lack motivation to actively explore the world; they will find it difficult to perceive and understand interrelationships or to remember and retain experiences they have had; they will struggle to notice and resolve social conflicts.

Secure attachment is the basis for children to play freely. Curiosity and pleasure, along with affirmation of what they are doing, are needed for them to discover and experiment with the capacities they bring with them into the world.

Phases of play in child development

A healthy child's play passes through certain phases. We can subdivide the first seven years into three rough sections that run parallel to physical, emotional and mental development. During these first seven years children reconfigure their inherited physical body, adapting it to their individual nature and disposition. All sensory impressions, like all early attachment experiences, shape brain development. Children are open, assimilating and imitative beings. They suck up sensory experiences like sponges, and these initial impressions are formative and lasting.

Play in babies and infants

Both babies and infants are preoccupied with getting to know the world and the things around them, and imitating these. Children acquaint themselves with the function of things in their surroundings through play, internalising actions and modes of behaviour they experience in daily life, and appropriating social behaviours. In so doing they learn about the world and the basic nature of interrelationships around them. Perceiving these relationships represents an important developmental step.

As soon as babies can focus their gaze, they play with their hands and fingers, putting them in their mouth and grasp hold of them – until eventually they can pick up an object. In the same way that they first explore their hands, babies then turn their attention to their own bodies and then to the objects that surround them.

The movement development that runs parallel to play

development demonstrates infants' joy and delight in their own actions. Every step in mobility development is repeatedly tried out until securely mastered. Young children do not wish to be diverted or disturbed, as they are involved in the serious – yet at the same time playful – pursuit of acquiring skills and capacities for their whole life.

This requires carers to observe and hold back, so as not to anticipate things prematurely. It may be hard for adults not to intervene when children only very slowly, by their own means, reach towards an object that lies beyond their grasp. If carers are too quick to help children, who may be crying or whining, their autonomy and will is weakened. While infants may have what they wanted, they will quickly lose interest and become ever more dissatisfied over time. This in turn makes parents uncertain and so – with the best intentions – they may try to please the child by offering another, and yet another, toy.

The capacity to connect with things and to immerse oneself in play, to develop interest, is formed in the first few years. The Hungarian paediatrician Emmi Pikler writes:

> It is important for children to discover as many things for themselves as possible. If we help them solve every task, we actually deprive them of the most important thing for their psychological development. A child who accomplishes something through independent experimentation gains quite different knowledge of things than one to whom a solution is offered on a plate.[28]

In the first three years, children take huge developmental steps: they learn to walk, speak and think, and these phases are reflected in their play.

Babies first get to know themselves and then explore their surroundings. Infants examine how things function, moving objects around. They throw things out of the buggy or pram then look radiantly at their mother in the hope that the object will reappear. They build towers and knocks them down, arrange rows of wooden blocks, build trains and line up all available toy cars in a row, delighting parents with their sense of order. They start to categorise objects with particular properties, acquiring the ability to make distinctions.

Children imitate symbolic actions that they observe in their surroundings, and discover spatial and causal laws and categories. They gather experiences about physical properties of the material world. In playing they learn to make functional use of objects.

In a next step, roughly between twelve and eighteen months, children have internalised their actions to an extent that allows them to apply them to new situations. At a meal time, for instance, they may put a spoon in their mother's mouth or offer their father something to drink. Subsequently these actions are transferred to play with a doll or teddy bear. As they develop, children imitate actions that are thematically connected – cooking for a doll, laying the table or driving a toy car into a garage. In all such play children are as yet tied to occurrences they have actually experienced or witnessed.

This changes in the second year, from roughly 21 to 30 months, as soon as children can visualise an object that is not present. From now on, a stool can become a motorbike, a ship or a car... Children start to release themselves from realistic images and to form their own inner pictures. This new phase of play begins when children acquire the capacity to say 'I' of themselves rather than referring to themselves by their given name. Ego development and play run parallel to each other.

Based on these insights, how do we organise the surroundings in which children under three play?

- Young children need a stimulating environment. They want to experiment and try things out, explore the world and get to know it. To do this, they need materials that can be played with in diverse ways and that are freely available to them.
- The play materials themselves should be comprehensible and accessible in nature. For instance, a ball with a bell hidden in it

may sound nice, but young children do not understand where the sound comes from.

- The carer or teacher should have a natural serenity, cheerfulness and pleasure in what is happening, which gives children the psychological space they need to develop and to engage with new things.
- Children need space to express their natural urge for movement: jumping, hopping, crawling, wriggling, pushing and carrying… all this strengthens them in different ways.
- Time is another important factor: children should have time to play, to explore their surroundings and connect with them, with the freedom to repeat certain actions until they have mastered them. Infants will endlessly practise taking the lid off a box and putting it on again, with rapt attention and great pleasure when they succeed.
- Children also need playmates of the same age, as well as the stimulus of older children.

Adults need to be psychologically present and available, to observe, support and, if necessary, protect children. For children to discover the world, carers must keep trying to find a balance between affirming them on the one hand and offering them new stimuli on the other.

Play in rising three to rising five-year-olds

From rising three to rising five, formative forces work strongly in children's rhythmic realm and on the rhythmic organs, the lungs and heart. All repetitions and rhythmic sequences nurture them and help foster healthy growth.

Children love little rituals and habits. Picture books and stories, songs and verses, cannot be repeated often enough. Children in kindergarten will often speak or sing along with rhythmic stories and poems, developing and nourishing their rhythmic memory.

Young children live within and love repetition. Just as a sequence of movements is tried out and repeated until children have fully mastered it, a story or ring game only really takes effect through regular repetition. We know from neurobiological research that the synapses form through continual repetition. A single impression is not enough to stimulate neuronal links in a child's brain.

Between the ages of two and three, imagination develops in play. Children can now act out roles creatively, often in rapid succession. Whereas before they often played *alongside* other children, and rarely looked for others to play with, they now meet other children with a new sense of self. Social *interplay* slowly develops, and younger children are accepted as play partners by older children. In starting to say 'I', they acquire a germinating sense of identity: children emerge from unity with the world into duality, and become self-aware.

At this new phase, everything available is incorporated into play. A building block changes from a mobile phone to an iron, and a child who was a dog a moment ago is the next moment a whale in the ocean. Play changes continually. Tidying up is very much of secondary priority. The 'chaos' that arises is their process of creation. Everything originates from their pictorial world in an inner process invisible to adults – except in the playthings that need tidying up.

Children now involve others in play as a matter of course, communicating with them and making social agreements. They learn to share play materials and sometimes to relinquish them. They learn to accept certain rules that form the external framework for their play. Children introduce their ideas into games, and construct the most adventurous buildings and aeroplanes using tables, play stands, chairs and cloths.

Play arises entirely from children's powers of imagination and creativity. These powers that originate in an inner world of pictures are now released to engage and connect with the outer world. Strings and ribbons, for instance, can be used in all kinds of ways: not just for tying things together but, say, as cables in an aeroplane or goggles for a deep-sea diver. This intense phase of imaginative play and role-play lasts from rising three to rising five.

Play between rising five and rising seven

Around the age of five, play changes again. For the first time in their lives, children may pass through a phase of boredom that can be regarded as preparation for the next play stage. The imaginative play and role-play of pre-school children is now strongly characterised by ideas.

Children will often arrive in the morning with detailed plans for play. They gather their friends together and give precise instructions on how and what games will be played. Rules are negotiated and adhered to. Children can now clearly distinguish between playing and reality. They might say, for instance, 'I'm going to pretend that I'm so and so, and you can be...' The initiator of the game is often also its leader. Play will last longer, perhaps taking the whole of free play time, and will often continue the following day. 'Come on, let's play circus,' the children might call out, and then they will plan it and work it all out.

Besides the many diverse skills children acquire in the first seven years, the three stages of development they pass through come to the fore in the way play develops. Just as the first years serve exploration of the world and growing familiarity with it, the step into duality – the second major milestone in play development – introduces new qualities. Children can now communicate with others in speech, learning to express feelings and developing social skills. They open up and broaden their psychological space. The third step opens up the world of ideas, and towards the end of the kindergarten period we see clearly how children can establish causal connections based on the physical and emotional experiences they have acquired in play. They are now ready for school.

Play environments for older children

An intentionally organised environment gives children stimulus for play and activity. The materials used should inspire the imagination without constricting it. Play materials in kindergarten stimulate creative play by giving children freedom. A simple toy, without too much detail, gives scope for imagination and creativity. Thus a simple rag doll can play many different roles, each with its own characteristics – beloved baby, cheeky child, loving mummy or joking daddy and so on.

The more detailed toys are, the fewer opportunities children have to actively create their games. Creativity is reined in, and the play materials themselves acquire far more predominance. This means, say, that children can no longer picture a car if the toy has no wheels, and seek ever more realistic images. This leads to dissatisfaction and agitation, since there are no demands on them to create their own pictures. It is understandable, therefore, if the toy is taken apart instead – a different kind of creativity.

The inner activity required to complement materials with few details, making them whole in the child's imagination, has a shaping and configuring effect on brain development.

In kindergarten, children should be allowed to build big, extensive structures. Besides plenty of play stands there are building boards and ladders; after asking, benches, chairs and tables can be used too. Playthings are usually made of natural materials and shaped organically to give children diverse sensory stimulus; seashells, stones, conkers, wooden bricks and so stimulate sensory-motor experiences. There is a big difference between children picking up a real stone and feeling its texture and weight, its warmth or coolness; and playing with an artificial stone (made of plastic or polystyrene). The latter does not offer an authentic tactile experience.

In Waldorf kindergartens, children are allowed free rein to improvise. Cloths and ribbons of all sizes and colours can be used in many different ways in play – as a costume for a princess or for building a house or cave. Materials are versatile enough to avoid games becoming pre-determined.

Besides objects used in play, the room's overall spatial and architectural design plays an important role. There are plenty of corners into which children can withdraw without always being subject to the teacher's scrutiny, recognising children's need to 'just be on our own'.

A friendly, lively atmosphere nourishes children's play. All craft and domestic activities, in which children follow an adult's example, offer them sensory experiences, and stimulate their activity and engagement. The teacher or carer's inner stance is key in a kindergarten group, and contributes vitally to an atmosphere of openness and freedom in which deep and satisfying play can unfold.

III

Waldorf Early Years Care in Practice

Waldorf Childcare Centres: Caring for Children Under Three

Birgit Krohmer

In recent decades, Steiner-Waldorf kindergartens have necessarily adapted to changes in society, and a range of early years care is now available. Kindergartens that used to offer morning provision now stay open all day. For a long time, it was inconceivable in Waldorf philosophy to admit children to kindergarten before the age of four, but now it is completely normal to accept them a whole year earlier, from three.[28] In many places there are groups for babies and infants under three, depending on country, location and government funding.

The tradition of the mixed age group kindergarten does not match the needs of the under-threes, so new educational ideals and quality guidelines were needed. Rudolf Steiner had many thoughts on the first three years of life, which must be seen in the overall context of human development. The challenge here was to relate detailed observation of children to the anthroposophic view of the human being, and from this derive specific guidelines for carers.

People sometimes ask whether Waldorf education is still up to date. As long as educational measures take full consideration of the reality of each individual child, and repeatedly relate this to a broader anthropology, they will not fail to work with actual children and their current needs. New tasks in education, such as extending provision to the under-threes, offer an opportunity to prove the value of our approach. Educational research that encompasses perception of the individual child's needs enables Waldorf education to remain relevant.

At the same time, of course, practice is enhanced and updated by the latest findings – such as the work of Hungarian paediatrician Dr Emmi Pikler, attachment research studies, or brain research. The empirical findings of Emmi Pikler can be read as a methodology for the kind of precise, unprejudiced Goethean observation Steiner urged educators to practise.[29] By different routes, both Pikler and Steiner arrived at the same results. In decades of shared work, this fruitful alliance has proven its worth, facilitating a professional approach that, in work with both parents and children, broadens the carer's skills and offers clearer guidelines.

Whenever family circumstances allow, it is more appropriate for children to grow, in familiar surroundings, into a limited and therefore clear family group before becoming acquainted with larger social communities. However, the current social trend is for both parents to work and to place children with extended family or in childcare provision. There are also many women – something that hasn't changed – who feel lonely and isolated at home, and who may therefore not provide the most nurturing environment for their children. As more fulfilled, working women they may actually be better mothers, so that the time they do spend together will be cheerful 'quality time'. The number of single parents has also risen drastically. Social changes mean that fathers are often more involved in childcare from the outset. Change always requires us to relinquish old habits, but at the same time offers an opportunity to develop new qualities.

Being together with other children in a group is a great challenge for infants, but it can also nurture new capacities. For many 'only children' this is also their sole opportunity to encounter other children. What was once first experienced amongst siblings – making allowances, learning to wait, observing other children and the way they relate to adults – can now be experienced in childcare settings.

Socialisation in this new type of group requires much presence of mind and attention from nursery carers. Children will repeatedly need intimacy, and often undivided attention from an adult, otherwise conflicts may develop between them. When first joining the group, these three phases can best help children find their way into their new circumstances:

- Initially children attach themselves to the adult responsible for helping them acclimatise.
- Once they have settled into the room with the adult's help, and familiarised themselves with the rhythm of the day, they can start to spend more time on their own.
- If they feel safe with their key attachment person and the normal rhythm of the day, their contacts can broaden to include other adults and children.

Up to the age of one, children are in their own space, though they often like being near another child. Initial relationships start to develop, such as passing toys back and forth. And of course a toy in another child's hand is much more interesting than an identical one lying on the floor next to you. Thus children make contact with each other.

From age one onwards, children form small groups, and by two the 'big ones' clearly have different needs in terms of social interaction and play. For children of rising three, carers need to develop the transition to kindergarten.

In this field, therefore, there is a diverse range of requirements, corresponding to children's various needs and involving each child's family. The child's experience is richer when both parents take responsibility for care, rather than the mother alone. Of course this takes more work since the principle of 'singing from one song sheet' can often be problematic in daily reality.

The task of kindergarten teachers and nursery carers has therefore broadened to include that of creating a protected space for early childhood, and tailoring care to each family's current needs. Below I want to detail some important aspects of working with young children, giving a glimpse of the work of Waldorf centres. Waldorf guidelines for birth to age three are already available.[30]

Development

Development can be seen as a movement between polarities. The more tangibly the two poles manifest, the more easily children can orient themselves and the more freely adults can attend to the moment of encounter.

The polarity between day and night is an archetypal rhythm. Newborn babies, initially cared for round the clock, can still experience the difference between the darkness of night, when things are done very quietly, and the brighter light of day, when talking, singing and so forth begin again. When we give a big yawn, this is the best 'explanation' of what phase of the day we're in. Many babies drink more calmly at night, swallowing less air, which shows that during the day, too, they will thrive better given less stimulus and changes of activity around them. Nowadays, however, sensory overload – both visual and acoustic – is normal, as soon as we leave the house, if not inside it.

Another rhythmic element differentiates between 'being on your own' and 'being with others'. This interplay, which becomes more predictable for children if they have a regular and reliable daily routine, has a confirming, consolidating and ordering effect, like the intake and digestion of food. The more intimate the time together – not just through breastfeeding, but also in the quality of encounter – the more satisfied and 'full' children will be. They will then be capable of being alone in a calmer way, and will be all the more alert and hungry the next time they are fed or attended to, paying closer attention to our facial expressions, gestures and words. Only children whose fundamental need for food, closeness, warmth, attention, real encounter and attachment are met will be happy on their own. They first explore their own body, then their surroundings, and after this start being active in them. Moments of peace and stillness allow them to attend to the noises and sounds they themselves make, and they will then follow the dialogue of other people with interest. The toy industry does not help here: the majority of baby toys rattle, clatter, play music or even 'talk', 'bleat' or 'moo'. But young children can only understand sounds that they can grasp hold of or see the source of; noises with no apparent sensory origin have less meaning. The more adults talk to children authentically in real dialogue, the more attentive and interested they will be in people. If the objects they play with are simple and understandable, and do not produce self-created noises, children will start to recognise and distinguish between animate and inanimate reality.

Exploring and taking hold of the body, exploring the world, and learning about relationships through adults are the essential needs of a young child's daily life. These require safe surroundings adapted to and appropriate for children's explorations and development, along with adults who sense intuitively when children need their attention or when they wish to try things out alone. Having their carer's undivided attention, initially in feeding, allows children to move on from having their individual needs met to incorporating the needs of a broader community. A child's model for social interaction is most decisively formed by the surrounding adults and the way they relate to the child and each other. The 'I and you' relationship can then grow into a sense of 'we'.

Phases of early childhood development

Rudolf Steiner highlights the polarity of head and limbs, and the centre that mediates and combines them. This principle of the human form is one he sees coming to expression in temporal phases of human development. He therefore acknowledges a threefold quality both in the human form and in developmental stages.[31]

In child and adolescent development we distinguish three seven-year periods, each of which has its own signal qualities:

- Imitation and example in the first seven-year period.
- Emulation and beloved authority in the second seven-year period.
- Ideals and the forming of values and judgements in the third seven-year period.

Figure 1: The three seven-year periods of child development.

Each of these periods can be further subdivided into three. These phases must be seen as general laws and patterns that vary individually with each child. Here I will look at a few aspects of the first seven years, in particular its first third.[32]

The disproportionately large heads of newborn children are immediately striking. Later on the trunk dominates, and towards school age arms and legs lengthen, and hands and feet grow. Corresponding to these growth phases, children inhabit each 'region' respectively, and reveal this in diverse ways.

How do babies hide? With a cloth or with hands covering their eyes they play 'peepo' with great pleasure, pulling the cloth away quickly to reveal themselves – and 'disappearing' again by pulling the cloth back over their face. When a little older, they love finding a tight, dark cupboard to hide in, or wrap themselves up in a curtain. Hiding means 'I feel myself in a narrow, dark space'. On emerging again, children will often leap into the adult's arms, and enjoy renewed pleasure of the 'we' experience in this contact. They will often say beforehand what they are about to do: 'Mummy, I'm going to hide in the cupboard. Will you come and find me?'

Towards school age, children are capable of preparing for a game of hide-and-seek by pushing boots under a long coat hanging in the cupboard to check whether the coat will hide them. When the child hides there will be no need to move anything, which might be a give-away for the 'seeker'. If not found, the child may keep the secret for future games.

Simple examples of this kind show how development proceeds from the head in infants to the trunk in four and five-year-olds through to a full, head-to-toe sense of self in pre-school children. Likewise, we find three clearly distinguished phases of play. Babies gather, link and combine all sensory impressions and experiences. They create a synthesis from their impressions. Everything is felt, crinkled, pressed, thrown, knocked, positioned, stood upright or made to move – depending on material and shape. Growing more agile over time, the hands adapt to the form of an object before they grasp it, so children can hammer, clatter and rotate a spoon in a saucepan. If an adult makes some reference to the child making a 'soup', the latter will usually look blank, since there is no 'soup' to be seen. The adult already assumes that the imagination is at work here, whereas in fact the child is still in the phase of 'functional play'. With good reason we call this the 'sensory-motor' phase. By the end of the first third of the first seven-year period, children have long passed the highpoint of explorative enquiry and now want to do as much as possible with us – a tiring phase!

One day a child may ask, 'I made apple sauce. Will you try it?' From now on we can barely tell whether children's imagination endows things with their reality, or whether the things themselves enchant children and, as it were, invite them to play. Let's imagine for a moment what it would be like if sticks, stones and leaves continually bewitched us – we would never keep to any schedule. The age of imagination, as it is called, has now arrived, and strikes parents and teachers as a fresh, burgeoning oasis. But as a permanent, lifelong condition, this phase of enchantment by vivid imagination would become a prison for us, rendering self-determination impossible.

A further milestone in development arrives when a child says, 'I'm bored...' Only now do children start planning games and making agreements, creating rules and roles and following through with them. They no longer say, 'That's my stove' but 'That could be my stove' – a giant step in consciousness! Freedom comes to expression here, even in the implicit subjunctive tense: 'I could do this and that and you could answer like this, and I would be this person or that...' The experiences of experiment and construction in play, along with imagination too, are now knowingly and intentionally employed.

In every developmental phase we can always observe a prelude followed by flowering or maturing and then fading, with marked transitions inbetween.

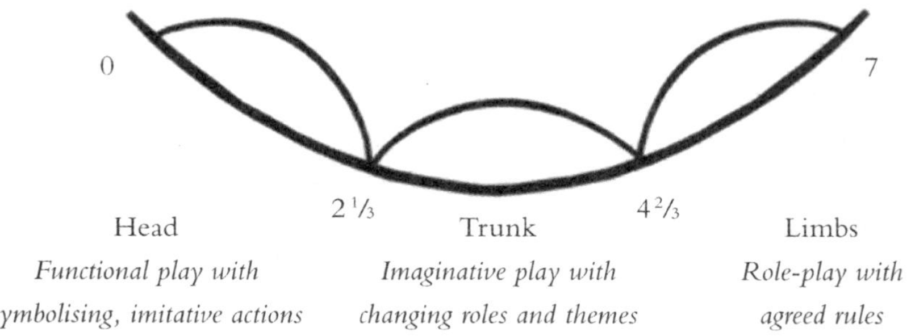

Figure 2: The three developmental phases in the first seven years.

First children take hold of the body and develop their body image. Then they explore potential movements and master surrounding space. They become familiar with objects and their nature, explore, examine, collect, sort or re-order them.

Within this period we find a further three-phase step:

1. Children engage with gravity as they pull themselves upright, and take hold of their body through to independent walking.
2. They learn to speak and become comfortable with dialogue and interpersonal exchange.
3. They independently configure and order thinking, which is expressed visibly in play and audibly in speech. None of us can say 'I' of ourselves through mere imitation, or 'you' to the other person. Between saying 'Paula is hungry' and 'I am hungry', the child has accomplished a vital process of internalisation and transformation.

We can see the expression of incipient independent thinking when children create their own, often charming, formulations. Here are some examples:

- Lisa experiences something new, which she lacks words to express. After her first play date with a friend, she says, 'He falled me.'
- Daniel was told the knife was too sharp for children to hold. He asked, 'Don't you have a gentle knife?'
- Equally typical is the age-specific statement, 'The tea has to un-heat; I can't drink it yet…' This is in fact far more accurate in physical terms than our way of putting it!

In Rudolf Steiner's accounts of child development, it is only in the first third of the first seven-year period that we find this further subdivision into three – of walking, speaking and thinking. The younger children are, the more subtle and defined is this subdivision. This also certainly matches our sense of time. Young

children can scarcely wait for their birthday tomorrow, or for Christmas Day, but the older they become the more easily they manage this. For adults, in contrast, time just flies by. To begin with, parents count their child's age in weeks or months. In almost all development schemas, the first year of life is described in the greatest detail, while later we refer to one-year-old, two-year-old or three-year-old children.

Figure 3 subdivides the first third of the first seven-year period into further phases.

Figure 3: Developmental phases in young children.[33]

The younger children are, the more often they need food and sleep. Slowly, waking hours become longer. Every child under three should be allowed to sleep undisturbed whenever tired, and also be able to withdraw from a group whenever necessary. Social skills grow when children feel good in themselves. Tolerance for frustration develops if children can experiment in an unimpeded way – rather than being subject to socialisation requirements or instructions. Children under three do not need a mini-kindergarten that prematurely introduces activities suited to kindergarten age. Premature measures at this age merely prevent children from settling and feeling fully comfortable in themselves. The role of carers is to give children necessary care and domestic attention, with conscientious goodwill and pleasure; craftwork and organised games have no place. Centred, grounded adults who enjoy what they are doing, but also take the time to be observant and attentive, give a wonderful example to children. A game of hand gestures or knee-riding may well be appropriate for a child who wants to sit on your lap for a moment in the morning. Any schedule that leads to time pressures and runs counter to children's own self-directed activity impairs development at this age.

A regular daily routine has an ordering effect on children's inner sense of structure. Consistency in every action also orders children's inner clock and thinking. Any rules must be ones adults themselves demonstrate and follow, and should not be wordily explained. Regularity develops into good habits, and in this way children settle increasingly into their environment with all its activities and sequences.

Washing hands before a meal, for example, can be an important event. Receiving the soap, children immerse it in water and it becomes slippery. Rubbing the hands makes suds and foam – what an experience! Then the soap is washed off and children can check if their hands are really soap-free. And isn't it amazing that the water always flows away when the plug is taken out of the basin! Simple things like these, which appear so trivial to us, make a different impression on each child and lead to further explorations. In professional development courses I sometimes get people to describe the different ways children wash their hands. In any team, everyone can always tell immediately which child is being described by the distinctive way this simple activity is performed.

Different models of childcare

The Waldorf approach now offers a range of provision for children under the age of three, from whole day nurseries to weekly parent and child groups, where parents can get to know each other, and discuss the many questions daily family life throws up. The length of the care session offered must match a family's actual situation and take account of the child's real needs. For example, it is preferable for children to be collected at the same time each day than never to know whether Daddy is coming before or after lunch, or before or after the afternoon nap. If parents trust carers, it may sometimes be better to leave children an hour longer than to rush to collect them and then take them to the supermarket on the way home. For family cohesion, it is good to spend as much time together as possible, but this should be in a relaxed atmosphere without time pressures or other commitments.

Irrespective of the form of childcare you choose, for children under three it is always important to create a protected, safe space in which they can be content on their own or with other children. This phase of childhood presents infinite challenges, and it may be very hard or impossible at a later age to correct issues that arise during this stage. It is therefore a great shame if kindergartens introduce things prematurely in these first three years. Their time will come! If we give serious credence to the transformation of etheric or formative forces throughout childhood development, it is clear that we must not institute a kind of mini-kindergarten at this young age. Instead we should seek to create a living space in which children can attach themselves to, and imitate, the adults around them. This is why younger children need a more differentiated physical environment and a smaller group size than kindergarten children. I will intentionally refrain from describing a 'typical' day in a childcare centre, since this depends on whether all children in a group can already walk or whether some are still lying, sitting or crawling; the age and stage of each child will mean different kinds of emphasis. The younger ones, for example, will usually have a nap both before and after lunch, while the older ones will have just one nap, usually after lunch. And after a bad night, the day may begin with a little morning nap. In every group individual children will have distinct, specific needs, which vary each day, so the course of each day will likewise be flexible. A saying by Friedrich Schiller characterises the mood adults can aim to foster in this situation: 'Seek for peace, but through repeatedly renewed balance, rather than standstill in your work.'

The mood in a group of young children depends greatly on the adults and their outlook. The more flexible the schedule, the more each person comes into their own: allowing them to create a homely, protective mood. I'd like to quote a few experienced carers speaking of what motivates them, because the quality of a care setting depends not foremost on its premises and equipment but on the people who work there.

> The most important thing for me is to study anthroposophic insights into human development. I observe how children learn to walk, speak and think in their own way. This enables me to gain an intuitive sense, informed by actual experience and always questioned anew, of the individual developmental needs of children entrusted to my care. The rhythm of the day in the protected space of the nursery has a healing effect, including on those with potential behavioural problems. The transition between activity and rest is one I myself demonstrate, and children can sleep whenever they feel the need. When I have changed four children's nappies, then have a break and sit on my chair just looking calmly around me, I help to create a comfortable atmosphere so that the children can feel centred and perceive their own needs.

> I like cooking, and I start each day by preparing vegetables. To begin with only one or two children will be there. They watch, chat with me or play around me – just as I did when I was at home with my own young children. When everyone enjoys the meal at lunchtime, I'm delighted! Sometimes people give us apples or plums and then I bake a cake.

> We go outside as much as possible, and this makes the children strong and healthy. At lunchtime they are really hungry, and they sleep well. Acclimatisation, dropping off and collecting are much simpler when our day starts and

ends in the garden. We usually only go inside for meals or to change nappies and have a nap.

In a society offering increasingly diverse lifestyles, there is no place for ideological constraints or the defence of narrow educational models or trends. All that matters is the well-being of each and every child. The younger the child, the more this encompasses the well-being of the whole family. Here, with its emphasis on working with parents, the Waldorf approach has much to offer. Stable key attachment figures in childcare centres, and a unified pedagogical approach, mean that children's lives are less disrupted by change when infant care, kindergarten and school strive at each age to maintain optimum conditions for a child-friendly childhood.

What do families today need? How can society help people find the courage to become parents? And how can parents find the support they need to enjoy their parenting? If adults convey a sense of malaise in coping with children or parenthood, it does not encourage children to enjoy their childhood, nor does it provide them with a secure foundation for their own subsequent parenthood. To communicate this pleasure in childcare is a great social task, for parents and educators equally.

Working with young children requires a special capacity to collaborate with other adults in silent agreement. The fewer 'programmes' there are, the more adults work in response to what children need at any and every moment, and the more parents and carers must agree clear guidelines in advance. Yet, when a situation demands it, we must have the flexibility and willingness to do everything in a different way from planned. Since young children live far more than we do in the atmosphere that surrounds them, they are like seismographs for unspoken nuances and undercurrents that we may not even notice. Mutual trust and acknowledgment in the team, and good collaboration between parents and care staff, create a secure foundation for imitative children. They will thrive when surrounded by a warm atmosphere of respect, regard and esteem. In infant pedagogy, therefore, the carer's professional profile widens to include working with the whole family, which in turn requires high levels of competency in inter-adult communication.

In anthroposophic infant pedagogy, a range of different training broadens the scope of mainstream training for this age. Infant pedagogy is currently being integrated into a broader training scheme. For young children particularly, who cannot yet articulate their own needs, it is essential that caregivers receive more extensive training. The best examples of an education that leads ultimately to freedom are adults who can decide and act for themselves in response to each new situation. Adults who know where they stand, exploring the possibilities offered by each situation and engaging honestly with their work, give children the psychological foundations for taking their developmental steps: from standing to understanding, from seeing to insight, and from grasping physically to an emotional and mental grasp of life.

For infants, only the best will do! Their future should be our deepest concern.

Daily Life in Waldorf Kindergartens: Educational Foundations

Marie-Luise Compani

Settling in to early years care: a first step towards independence

After the birth of their first child, parents often wonder how they can both pursue their careers and find good quality childcare. In their research of the facilities on offer, open days will give them a sense of the range of options and educational outlooks.

Having discussed basic provision, parents must consider whether their child's needs will be fully met. Will each child receive adequate care and attention as part of a group? How will a child cope with the transition between home and childcare? What will the effect be on the child's development? It is especially important for many parents that their children socialise with other children from a young age.

These concerns are discussed and considered in admission interviews, which allow the opportunity for mutual dialogue and exchange of information, so that parents can feel confident about placing their children where they will feel happy. If parents find a kindergarten with a warm, friendly atmosphere, where both child and parents feel accepted, a first bridge is built.

As the time for starting childcare approaches, there may still be anxieties and concerns about the imminent change. Separation is painful for many mothers and fathers: they are entrusting unknown hands with their precious child, without knowing exactly what will happen or how things will go.

It is not usual in Waldorf kindergartens to have 'taster days' during regular sessions. But introductory parents' evenings or afternoon meetings enable parents to become familiar with the premises, the daily schedule and the usual way things are done, and make their first contact with other mothers and fathers – who will usually answer their pressing questions and relate their own experiences.

Just before a child joins a group, settling-in measures and attendance times are discussed and agreed individually with the parents. Children's attachment to their families must always be taken into account, and sufficient time taken to introduce them to kindergarten, so that parents can pursue their jobs and activities in confidence, without worrying. Children who have already attended other childcare provision also need a settling-in period; likewise children making the transition from an infant care group to a kindergarten group. In this regard, acclimatisation guidelines are helpful to parents.

For young children about to be admitted to a nursery, it is advisable to ensure they have sufficient time with parents for them to retain clear orientation and reassurance about their primary attachment. This acclimatisation model therefore assigns great importance to including parents in the process, allowing children to slowly detach from mother and father while gradually forming a relationship with a specific nursery keyworker.

The settling-in process can sometimes last up to three weeks. Success depends on carers and parents working closely together in the initial phase, and discussing with each other how to handle the next step, until children feel secure in their new attachment.

This settling-in period is particularly important for admission of children under three. However, it should be carried out for every child, irrespective of age. Every new step presents children with new surroundings, and therefore represents an initial 'step back' in development, which children can overcome if accompanied with empathy and understanding by parents, carers and teachers.

Attending a childcare facility or kindergarten is a step towards a child's independence, and likewise calls strongly on developing powers of socialisation.

This means that children:

- have to manage without the help of parents.
- relinquish their individual rhythm to accommodate the group rhythm.
- are exposed to more, and to more intense, stimulus.
- have to settle in to new surroundings.
- have to enlarge the circle of key attachment figures, and no longer be the focus of all activity.
- have to find their place within the group and develop relationships with other children.

If this step is jointly, attentively and empathically accompanied by parents and childcare providers, it will form a sound foundation for subsequent kindergarten years. This applies in particular to all agreements made during the settling-in phase. We owe it to children to keep our word. Nothing is worse for children than to notice that they are not being told the truth, and that adults are not being authentic in their actions. It is also important for children to see that their pain about detaching and separating from parents is acknowledged. It is simply a sad moment, and it will help children to show that we understand this.

There are some signs that can tell us whether children have acclimatised, which include:

- They are happy to come to kindergarten (or nursery or playgroup) and can detach from their parents. This does not mean there will never be tears.
- They can engage in activities and start to play.
- They speak to their new carer.
- They explore the new premises and make contact with other children.

Attachment as foundation for education

Secure and reliable attachment to the new keyworker gives children the peace to develop at their own speed. To make this possible, Waldorf childcare centres uphold the principle of assigning each child a place in a stable group. In whole-day facilities, we avoid staff changes that alternate between morning and afternoon shifts.

It is important for children's security and confidence to feel at home in their group. They can depend upon having their key attachment figure and regular playmates around them. They live in a reliable context of relationships. If a change does occasionally occur, their world does not fall apart since they feel comfortable with the stable group, the premises, and the regularity of the daily, weekly and yearly rhythm. These things give them security and self-confidence.

In this way we enhance primal security and draw on children's innate trusting nature. They want to get to know the world through all their senses and gain their own experiences of it; they wish to learn how the world works, and they can only do so when they feel a secure sense of trust that they are accepted and loved, initially in their parents, and then later in other key figures. Living in a secure attachment means that children are safely harboured, whatever storms may rage, and this secure attachment is an indispensible condition for education.

Positive acclimatisation to childcare is therefore an important basis for a successful experience. Equally important, though, is for carers to cultivate relationships with parents and families. Secure parents gladly entrust their children to childcare centres, turn to them with their questions and concerns, and can make a decisive contribution to their child's positive experience.

'All education is self-education': the formative power of the individual

Besides professional competency, which must include trained insight into children's physical, mental and spiritual development, the stance and outlook of the carer or teacher who looks after children during this phase are decisive factors for the success of childcare. Educators must lead by example, by being involved in a process of learning, and providing children with a loving and secure context for relationships, while at the same time acknowledging them as individuals: this is the basis for education.

In his short, groundbreaking text, written in 1907, *The Education of the Child from the Perspective of Spiritual Science*,[34] Rudolf Steiner speaks of the two 'magic words' that apply to the first phase of a child's life (roughly up to the age of seven). They are 'example' and 'imitation'. These two words say something fundamental about the nature of the mutual relationship between young children and adults.[34]

Everything that occurs in young children's surroundings not only affects their psychological and mental development but also their bodily development, exerting a positive or negative influence even on the way their internal organs function. Besides purely physical or material factors in their environment, the inner stance and outlook of carers also decisively affects children. They intuitively sense whether they are loved and accepted as they are – with all their individual inclinations, gifts, idiosyncrasies and weaknesses – or whether carers feel frustrated by their distinctive nature. Children will reflect adults' inner stance back to them, which can make carers aware of their limitations and highlight the importance of their own example.

This 'example effect' extends through all areas of life, both in children's immediate surroundings and in their carers' personal qualities. This requires us to develop a high degree of self-reflection and self-education. For example, an adult who is a perfectionist signifies for young children a constriction of their own creative capacities. Alongside all professional skills, therefore, the carer or teacher must always try to be aware of 'blind spots' and failings. This offers a great opportunity for self-improvement, for working on our weaknesses.

Making an effort to redress things that have gone wrong is enormously fruitful in the educational process. Children experience these efforts and see that the adult is learning too, and this has an exemplary effect on them. A teacher striving to develop new qualities acts at a much deeper level than teaching children things. Consistency and congruent action means reliability and security for children. An adult's honesty and openness strengthens their sense of trust and confidence.

Attentiveness, respect and sensitivity create the basis for authentic interest in children and their family background, and allow teachers to play an active part in child development. Reverence for each individual child enables us to notice as yet hidden capacities that may be seeking expression. And educators or carers can feel gratitude for the privilege of accompanying and supporting children.

Humour, however, is also important for balancing serious effort; it introduces joy and lightness into daily kindergarten life. Children live in the here and now, and the teacher needs great presence of mind to respond to them. Perceiving interactions between different children and related group dynamics, kindergarten teachers can intervene to support and help where necessary. Or, if the situation allows, they can step back and look on as a quiet observer.

Rudolf Steiner tells us:

> Joy in and with one's surroundings is therefore another of the powers that have a formative effect on [the child's] physical organs. The teacher should have a cheerful look and outlook, and above all demonstrate authentic, unforced love for the children.[35]

This is a tough demand and a big responsibility, and can make us wonder how we can fulfil it on a daily basis.

In a cheerful, unforced and light-hearted atmosphere, which

arises from basic trust, children's confidence in their surroundings, and in their teachers or carers, will grow. Children feel at home in a mood that radiates emotional warmth and safety, and this also affects their physical growth and health. A fundamental atmosphere of this kind does not arise by itself, but requires adults to be continually aware of their own actions. *What* you do is far less important than *how* you do it. Inner involvement in activities is important, even in something seemingly mundane like preparing the break-time meal or washing up. All such activities can be undertaken with interest and pleasure, and the satisfaction this emanates stimulates children and makes them feel at home. Kindergarten teachers must make daily efforts to create a development-nurturing environment of this kind.

Rudolf Steiner summarises the most important underlying aspect of education, and thus also kindergarten work, as follows:

> All education is self-education, and as teachers and carers we are in a sense just the environment of the self-educating child. We must provide the most beneficial environment so that children can educate themselves through us in the way that accords with their own inner destiny.[36]

The strengthening power of rhythm

'Lettuce leaf, lettuce leaf, lettuce leaf the whole year through, in January, in February, in March and April too…' A children's rope-skipping verse. But why, some people might wonder, so monotonous in content? Leaving aside its possible meaning, it demonstrates two elements that inform daily life in Waldorf kindergartens: it has rhythm and repetition.

Rhythm and repetition are two sustaining factors in every child's daily life. We can see this very clearly in a newborn child who must first settle into a rhythm. Naturally it takes a while to establish a healthy sleeping and waking rhythm, and adults also have to help ensure this happens. Once a rhythm has been established, the whole family breathes more easily, as life can unfold in an ordered way once more.

Young children need an appropriate rhythm in order to 'settle' into the world, and this rhythm will vary a great deal individually. This individual rhythm will again change when children start to attend a childcare facility, where they will experience new rhythms of daily activity.

Just as alternating between day and night largely determines life, so phases of activity and rest punctuate the course of the day and render it rhythmic. The week, too, is rhythmically ordered. And the year, likewise, is strongly informed by seasonal and festival rhythms. This principle of life is an important element in Waldorf kindergartens, and attending to rhythm and repetition is intrinsic to its educational outlook. The day, week and year are rhythmically configured and thus become part of children's experience.

A really good rhythm is distinguished by the swing back and forth between two polarities, and its recurrence, like easy breathing, which sustains, enlivens and does not exhaust us. This contrasts with a strict, constricting schedule. The kindergarten day is divided into phases in which the children can play freely, shaping their own activity, followed by others of rest, absorption and calm – for instance at story time, meal times and rest times.

Naturally the group rhythm always takes its lead from the age of the children, and the nature of each group. Daily and weekly routines can vary a great deal, and are never uniformly dictated. They are adapted to children's particular needs. Before the age of three, children need a different routine from four or five-year-olds; and a child approaching school readiness likewise needs a different routine again. Different kinds and compositions of groups take this into account.

But why is a rhythmically ordered routine so important? Isn't it boring to play, eat breakfast or have a nap at the same time each day? In the familiar comprehensibility of rhythm and repetition children experience security, safety and reliability. This enhances the powers of growth and vitality they so greatly need for their physical development in the first seven years.

A child's will is always dependent on recurring external stimulus and is strengthened by establishing good habits. Daily actions such as cleaning teeth, brushing hair and washing hands are easiest to establish if they become a self-evident part of the daily rhythm. An old German proverb puts it very simply and clearly: 'What is not learned by little John, big John nevermore will learn.' Learning things as an adult that were not cultivated in early childhood takes considerably more energy and determination.

Children only slowly grow into a sense of time. Initially they live in the here and now: past and future lie beyond their grasp. During the first seven years they gradually come to an experience of tomorrow and yesterday, and a rhythmically ordered sequence of the day helps develop this. At a certain point they will no longer ask their kindergarten teacher when Mummy is coming for them. The continually repeated sequence of events in the day means they can rely on the fact that, after story circle and a little verse or farewell song, it will be 'home time'.

During these first seven years young children learn things 'bodily', with head, heart and hand. In the first kindergarten year they settle into the daily rhythm of the group. Initially they relate most strongly to the sequence of the day, for the week is as yet mostly beyond their grasp.

Before long, however, young children learn to distinguish the different events and activities of the week, such as: outing day, painting day, baking day or eurythmy day. This can be supported outwardly by the sequence of meals through the week, so that each day is experienced bodily, as well as through activities. When children arrive at kindergarten in the morning, the aromas of whatever is cooking will already tell them what day it is: 'Oh, today is porridge day!' they might call out, and 'Yes! And it's eurythmy day!' Usually they will soon get a sense of what day of the week it is; and the older ones, approaching school age, will put it more directly: 'It's Wednesday.'

The larger rhythms of the year are shaped by seasonal activities in spring, summer, autumn and winter, by celebrating festivals. Engagement with the powers and cycles of nature repeatedly occurs through children's own, direct experience – such as sowing corn in spring, its growth and ripening in late summer, and harvesting in autumn, along with practical accompanying activities such as baking bread or making jam. Season-appropriate ring games and songs – describing, say, the sowing of seed and the growth of plants – raise these experiences to an artistic realm in children's psyches. Through their own activity and experience, therefore, they can connect strongly with the cycle of the seasons.

The celebration of seasonal festivals also creates highlights in the rhythm of the kindergarten year. The whole process, including preparations, the celebration itself and reflection afterwards, should be one children can themselves engage in and clearly grasp. [37]

While young kindergarten children will just look on in wonder as preparations for a festival get underway, older children will follow it all with great interest and try to help where they can. Approaching school age, children have a clearer sense of what is involved in each particular festival. And so, throughout the kindergarten period, children's perspective continually broadens as they increasingly connect with the culture around them. They settle into a daily rhythm, develop a sense of the course of the week and, through recurring festivals, form a relationship with the repeating cycle of the seasons.

Little rituals and customs are also cultivated and repeated on a daily basis. Young children, as we have seen, live in and love repetition. Just as they will repeatedly practise a movement or set of movements until they have mastered them, they get to know a story or ring game through continual repetition, which they never find boring. In Waldorf kindergartens, a ring game, fairy tale or story will be repeated over a period of two to four weeks. This time frame supports children's desire for repetition, and repetition in turn strengthens development of rhythmic memory.

The principle of repetition should not be confused with a

fixed schedule. The moment an activity or action lapses into programmatic routine, it loses its living quality and has a hardening effect. Children sense this very quickly and reflect it in their behaviour. When a ring game or fairy tale recurs each year, the teacher needs to refresh and re-enliven it as if the children were hearing it for the first time.

We know from neurobiological research that the synapses in children's brains only develop through continual repetition. A single impression is not enough to stimulate neuronal networks. I once witnessed a child of fifteen months preoccupied with three stones over a six-week period. During this time the stones were his favourite toy and continual companions! He took them everywhere, bringing them to nursery, taking them to lie down with him at rest time, and back home again in his coat pocket. This was an intense period of exploring and bonding, without the slightest trace of boredom. The child continually and quietly studied the stones' surfaces, weight, smell and much more.

It really makes a great deal of sense to tell a story, or act out a ring game, for two to four weeks. The powers of memory and will, along with the structures of the human organism, are not developed by showering young children with ever new impressions, however well intended this may be. Regularity of the day and intentional repetition enhance development by helping create a healthy bodily, emotional and psychological foundation.

And so we come back to – 'Lettuce leaf, lettuce leaf, lettuce leaf the whole year through, in January, in February, in March and April too…' – but not in strict adherence to a fixed routine. The art of creating a rhythm that nurtures and enlivens children lies in the continual, breathing recurrence of similar events.

A rhythm oriented to children's needs supports their healthy development, strengthens their vital forces and helps them to live their way into the world and connect meaningfully with it.

Preparing for school readiness in kindergarten

How do we shape the transition to formal schooling?

How the transition should be made between a Waldorf kindergarten or childcare centre and a Waldorf primary school is a question that often arises in discussions about school readiness. Each child will be carefully observed and monitored during the kindergarten years, and teachers, will be in regular contact with parents, prioritising discussion of their child's development. Development is documented and discussed at least annually with parents. This makes more work for carers and teachers but it produces a comprehensive picture of the child. Parents welcome such discussions and give extremely positive feedback about this opportunity to discuss their child.

In the course of the kindergarten period, therefore, an educational partnership between parents and teachers should arise to nurture children's well-being and shape their ongoing care. In addition, examination by the school doctor can contribute to a broader picture.

Teachers at the child's kindergarten and at his or her future school should collaborate and discuss the child's development in the last year of kindergarten, to make the transition as smooth as possible. The aim of this intensive monitoring is both to strengthen the child's capacities and abilities and to recognise any potential support and remedial needs in good time.

The phenomenon of boredom

What distinguishes children approaching school age? What bodily, emotional and psychological changes occur, and how do these become apparent in children's behaviour?

Children are now usually between five and six years old and

engaged in a process of change affecting their body and shape. They are often taller when they return after the summer holidays: their arms and legs are lankier, and their limbs longer; they start to look less like young children. Their voice grows stronger. Second dentition will be starting in some, or have already begun. The molars emerge and the first milk teeth fall out. Children will often complain of vague stomach aches, and in general we may notice their loss of enthusiasm. As their shape starts to change, they lose some of their physical, emotional and psychological equilibrium.

This can be a difficult phase for many children. Boredom and listlessness appear. Prior to this, children are rarely bored, but fully occupied in play or other activities. But now they may be reluctant to come to kindergarten, and this can greatly unsettle parents, who may think it is high time for formal school; that their child is bored and kindergarten no longer answers his or her needs. Kindergarten teachers will also notice the change, and hear children saying things like, 'I don't know what to do!' This is a sign that changes are afoot.

But what is the meaning of boredom for children approaching school age? It confronts them with themselves; they become ever more conscious and increasingly aware of their own bodies, hearts and minds. They start to compare themselves with others, and to assess their accomplishments. From one day to the next their kindergarten teacher can then, suddenly, be 'really stupid', or the children may plan together how to avoid rules and routine. Daily chores are questioned, and boundaries tested. These are signs of approaching school-readiness, and boredom will pass if parents and teachers know how to respond. It can be very troublesome, but it is worth simply waiting until children take the initiative again through their own resources, and engage once more. There is little point in showering them with all sorts of suggestions and choices.

Giving older children additional challenges

What children actually need in the year before they start formal schooling are challenges and tasks that tax their skills and allow them to sense their own limits. They still need the steady rhythm of the kindergarten day, which gives them security and safety. And they need acknowledgment and support alongside interaction with children of their own age.

Some children are intellectually precocious for their age and already literate and numerate before they go to school. Others are still very dreamy and playful; they are self-contained, live in their imagination in free play and prefer avoiding challenges. Then there are those who gladly accept tasks and chores, or care for the younger children in the group and engage eagerly and assiduously in every activity.

Children in their last year of kindergarten have varying skills and needs. While they may be looking forward to going to school after the summer holidays, they still enjoy the familiarity and safety that kindergarten provides.

In mixed age groups, children in their last kindergarten year grow into their new role. They are an example to the younger children in the group. As well as participating in normal daily and weekly kindergarten life, with baking, painting, eurythmy, outings etc., they are given additional things to do. These may lie either in the realm of gross or fine motor skills, such as sewing and embroidering, woodwork or felting. All these things require both finger dexterity and stamina. An extra outing may be provided for the older age group alone, or they may be offered movement sessions. Part of this phase also involves recognising that 'I can't always be the best' at every activity.

Within the group, the children approaching school age meet challenges in the social and emotional realm. They learn to consider others, recognise their own strengths, and help younger and less able children. They take on small tasks and can complete them. In the garden or on outings they test their skills in climbing and balancing, or seek out a quiet, secret spot to hide themselves from adult scrutiny. The nature of their movement becomes more differentiated and is now related to challenges, both in free play and ring games. In free play the oldest children become the leaders, introducing their ideas and plans, assigning roles and materials and continuing their games over a longer period.

It is a good idea to assign these older ones additional domestic jobs, such as helping a teacher prepare a meal or bake a cake. Such activities are a normal part of the kindergarten day, but there is a difference between preparing muesli together in the whole group and getting just a few of them to cook something for the others. The big ones help in a more focused way in the garden, sowing grass seed, planting flower bulbs, pruning branches or twigs and carrying them away to the chopping block and compost heap. In the group they take responsibility for the youngest children, tying their shoelaces for them and helping them put on their coats.

They can take on more challenging roles in ring games, too, or help the teacher to present a simple puppet show by moving the puppets. They take on these tasks gratefully and proudly, and no longer find the puppet show 'boring'.

Growing into these new tasks lasts roughly from the start of the new kindergarten year through to the Christmas holidays. After this, the future schoolchildren need even more challenges. They progress from simple sewing to projects such as making pincushions, puppets, dolls, ships, houses etc., and will continue with these until the summer holidays begin. They need concentration and persistence to complete these tasks, as well as dexterity, fine motor skills, a creative eye and proper handling of tools. After about twenty minutes their concentration is usually exhausted, and the work is left to one side until the following day. In the process, children experience their own strengths and weaknesses. They take on tasks and responsibility, and are proud of the things they achieve.

But here, too, the provision should remain varied to allow for the differing skills and needs of these older children. There is no absolute requirement for such projects. There may well be children who now, at the end of their time in kindergarten, can still throw themselves into play with enthusiasm and concentration. Despite all the serious focus and eagerness they may bring to their 'schoolchildren projects', such projects should not be overvalued. In general, the 'almost schoolchildren' take ever greater pleasure in play the closer they come to the end of their kindergarten period.

The example provided by the older children in mixed age groups is a fundamental part of kindergarten pedagogy. However, it is equally important for these pre-school children to be offered the chance to engage with each other without the younger ones. The scope of activities in kindergarten provides many creative possibilities for this, dependent, of course, on each centre's facilities and staffing. The important thing is to develop the skills of these older children, as well as recognising any remedial needs.

In the first seven years children acquire basic human capacities: in standing and walking they learn to orientate themselves in the world and take hold of it; in acquiring speech they enter into contact with the world and explore it; in learning to think they acquire the ability to understand the world. But all these things involve an unconscious, implicit process: children acquire and learn these skills bodily, with all their senses. At the end of this phase of development the forces that were active in growth have transformed and children become ready for school. Now they can focus on a task for longer and want to learn to read, write and count so they can master the world.

Starting formal schooling at the earliest possible age is, therefore – as studies have shown – not the best start to a school career. It is far better to allow children to engage in unhurried growth and sensory maturation, so that when they start school they are ready to do so with a healthy sense of self-reliance and self-awareness.

Real-Life Activities in Waldorf Kindergartens

Freya Jaffke

It is a great challenge for Steiner-Waldorf kindergarten teachers to introduce real-life activities and carry them out with children. It is not a matter of *demonstrating* an activity, such as baking cakes or bread, and reflecting with them on this. Instead, the children should participate unconsciously in the adult's work, experiencing the diversity, richness and imperatives of daily life. Above all, though, such work should awaken impulses in children that flow into meaningful, creative play; instead of following directions for an activity or game, their own will, expressed in imitation, is kindled, emerging freely and engaging with the world in a unique way.

Rudolf Steiner describes this as follows:

> So the task for the kindergarten is to introduce the work and activities of real life in such forms that they can flow out of the child's activity into play. We must guide life, the work done in life, into the work of the kindergarten[...].[38]

While fully engaged in their work, adults must at the same time observe the children. This isn't easy. The better this works, though, the more harmoniously children play; one can sense that they feel happy and safe in such a cheerfully diligent and unpressured atmosphere.

Before we look at individual ideas of work that can be done, let us consider broader types of activity and examples from daily experience with children.

Types of activity

We can divide the diverse kinds of work into four types:

Caring for children's surroundings

This includes organising and cleaning all the rooms the children use – from dusting, caring for the seasonal nature table and watering flowers, through to organising cupboards and their contents. Care of the garden (if there is one) and the area around and outside the house also belongs here.

Cooking and domestic tasks

This includes preparing small meals for morning break, baking bread, cakes etc., chopping, preparing or preserving fruit and sometimes herbs, doing laundry, washing, ironing and mending.

Making and looking after toys

'Making toys' refers to all hand-sewn dolls, puppets, gnomes, woolly sheep, and simple embroidery work – such as doilies, pincushions, tablecloths for the doll corner or the birthday table. Likewise various kinds of woodwork and woodcarving, such as small spoons or bowls for the doll corner, scoops for the shop stands, candle holders for both children's and dolls' birthdays and festivals, 'train carriages' made from pieces of wood with the bark on, bark ships, small horses and carriages. Likewise sawing branches into construction pieces, then sanding, waxing and polishing them, and weaving little baskets.[39]

'Looking after toys' includes caring for all toys made of wool, cloth, wood or bark that need regular care by washing, darning, mending of parts that have come loose. Wooden objects need occasional cleaning, and little repairs will be needed, such as mending a broken children's broom or a cracked wooden bowl.

Festival preparation

With a few exceptions during Advent and Christmas, almost all the work of preparing for festivals can be done in the children's presence. This can include: braiding a harvest wreath and tying little corn bunches for the harvest festival; painting and gluing lanterns for the lantern festival; setting up table stages for puppet shows; making an Advent wreath, dipping candles, making candle holders out of clay, making small tissue-paper transparencies, modelling small crib figures in beeswax and baking Christmas biscuits; decorating the room for Carnival; sewing Easter grass, painting Easter eggs and making little Easter bunnies from larch cones or wool; making Whitsun doves and butterflies from coloured wool; making various small items for the summer festival, such as flying balls, little bark ships with sails, and coloured bunting with crepe paper to demarcate play areas.[40]

Aspects of work

What is the distinctive nature of these activities, and how or where do the types of work referred to above arise?

Let us first describe a few examples of situations drawn from kindergarten practice.

The bird table needs a new roof

On a warm autumn day the teacher sits in the garden wearing a sunhat and work apron, close to the sandpit in which and around which children are playing. Next to her, on a small table, is a toolbox, and on the ground a large box of straw. With the garden scissors the teacher cuts the straw to the right length. In the process either shorter or longer pieces fall into the children's basket, from which they are allowed to take anything. A five-year-old boy sticks lots of stalk pieces together and then, after much effort, places them on the sand as parallel train tracks. He uses a piece of wood as a locomotive. His younger friend tries to copy him, but a loose stalk husk is hanging down from the second piece he takes, and he is very pleased to find he has a fishing rod. Two girls have made a flowerbed beside the sandpit. With the garden scissors they cut small sections of straw and use these to make a fence around their garden by sticking them in the sand. Another girl has discovered that she can use her piece of straw to blow sand off a board. A few children stand or sit beside the teacher, gather bundles of straw and pass them to her.

Children come and watch for a while to see how the teacher pulls fine wire through the holes in the bird-table roof board, on which straw and wooden dowelling are fixed. This work takes three days to complete. The whole time, the teacher must look beyond her work to the children playing all around: in the sandpit, by the conker tree – where a bottle train has been invented – to the children building a den with boards and branches, and those who are rope skipping or playing with balls, or engaged in other activities.

Making puppets

The teacher is making puppets for the end-of-year puppet show. He sits at the sewing table with silks, scissors, a pincushion, thimble and balls of thread, along with the children's basket and wool basket. Before long, children come to join him. There are always little baskets standing ready for them, into which they put children's scissors, pincushions, thimbles, thread and a piece of material from the cloth drawer. Naturally they always look into the children's basket to see what off-cuts are there, which may inspire them. It takes many days before the finished puppets hang ready on their hooks. And each day children come to sew in whatever way they can, or to play with thimbles and buttons. Now and then children need help threading a needle or cutting a piece of cloth the right size for a doll they have made themselves, or to tie a knot at the end of the thread. Children play whenever they wish or when they have had enough of sewing.

By the time the puppets are finished, two children have also made puppets, all by themselves. The younger of the two, who is just five, has made a little head with a cloak and a thread coming out of the top. The other, who is almost six, has made clothes for her puppet and attached all three threads to the head – one on the top and two on each side – as she does not yet understand their function.

Preparations for the Christmas market

- The teacher has sewn a series of shepherds over many days. Some children make their own little copies of them, in their own way. Now and then one of the children places something he has made into the box and says, 'For your stall.' Subsequently little sheep are made of wound wool (without using a felting needle). Someone in the room is talking about the Three Kings. Meanwhile a five-year-old boy is sitting at the sewing table in deep concentration, murmuring, 'Caspar, Melchior, Baldbazaar.'[41]

In the school workshop seven fathers have sawn up branches delivered by municipal gardeners, and sanded the cut surfaces;

these will be building materials. One box after another of these sawn pieces is brought into the kindergarten, and they are sorted into groups by size with the children's eager help. Then all available tables are covered with cloths and the pieces of wood spread out on them in roughly equal batches. The six-year-olds particularly do this conscientiously and with great pleasure. Over the coming days the sawn surfaces are rubbed with beeswax, polished, and each batch is packed away in a large box. On the top is placed a shoe box containing 'treasures': a bark ship with sail, little felt gnomes, various pine cones, stones, shells and acorn cups.

On one of the following days, a few mothers come to kindergarten first thing in the morning to help with the final preparations. Unspun sheep's wool is weighed at one table, packed in bags and labelled with a price. At another table the last few children's leather purses are finished with a fastening button and strap. At another, frames of gold cardboard are being cut for coloured transparencies. Meanwhile, shared break is being prepared in the kitchen corner.

There is a very busy, creative atmosphere, enfolding the children as they play. Some stop to help at one table or another, if they can, or use off-cuts of gold cardboard to fashion a crown for a doll or a star.

The above examples aim to show that it is of primary importance to create an atmosphere in which children in a mixed age group can freely settle and develop. Within this, every child can take individual learning steps at their own pace, without having to be told what and how to do something. Naturally, help is always given when necessary.

A working atmosphere of this kind succeeds when teachers do their work tranquilly. It is important for adults to choose a place where they can see everything that is going on in the room, and to equip it with everything they need both for themselves and for any children who wish to come and join in. It is also good to wear the right clothes for a job, for example, an apron. This gives outer credibility to the work being done. At the same time an inner truthfulness is important – accomplishing work with focus and pleasure – and encouraging children's play with the odd helpful or imagination-stimulating word.

Teachers' whole attitude and outlook to their work becomes apparent in their gestures. They should use tools with as much skill as possible, but it is also fine for children to see them having trouble with and having to overcome something; for example, making proper use of a thimble when sewing. We should not underestimate the significance of children witnessing our efforts as adults – our patience and persistence in overcoming problems – for this is something they unconsciously imitate.

When a task continues over several days – and this is only during the time remaining in the morning after daily chores, while the children play – children experience a beneficial sense of continuity and of familiarity. Larger projects, such as wood carving or embroidery, can extend over several weeks and create phases of activity that recur each year in connection with a particular season.

It is interesting to see how children relate to adults who are busy working. Some will watch or make something of their own, or serve the adult something to 'eat' or 'drink' from their 'café'. Or they may build a den right next to grown-ups because they wish to be their neighbour, or phone them on a self-made cellphone etc. During a period of wood carving, 'apprentices' will repeatedly appear to sweep up the wood shavings – if other children have not already taken these to 'cook' with, or to 'feed the horses'.

The work described here is incorporated into the adult's weekly rhythm of other activities, such as bread baking, setting up tables for watercolour painting, and cleaning and polishing the toy shelves and tables at the end of the week. In former times, mothers often drew up a weekly schedule of housework – for instance, laundry on Monday, ironing on Tuesday, darning on Wednesday, shopping on Thursday, cleaning on Friday and baking on Saturday. Teachers in kindergarten likewise have their recurring work schedule, which gives orientation to the children so that they learn the days of the week and their sequence in a natural way.

A schedule of this kind, though, is primarily for the adult. The children are quite free to join in or to play on their own or in groups. One should take care that the adult's work does not become the sole focus of children's activity. There are always some children who find it difficult to imitatively transform experiences they have at home or in kindergarten into their play. Their will is better strengthened if they find their own way into play, or discover an activity to pursue happily. They may often need help in doing so.

Besides focusing on their work, kindergarten teachers are of course entirely there for the children. Now and then they will put down their work: for instance, if candles are to be lit for a doll's birthday cake; if children have arranged a puppet show and ask the adult to tell the story; if a quarrel starts or if some danger threatens, say in building a large den. At any moment the teacher may also need to comfort or help a child.

Teachers will also always take time if individual children are in the process of learning something new. For instance, a six-year-old girl in my group had cut out some long strips of cloth, placed them over the head of a simple rag doll, and tied them with string. She wanted the doll to have not just hair but plaits. She came to me and asked, 'Can you show me how to plait?' After watching for a while she learned to plait and unbraid the hair as often as she liked.

A girl, just six, asked her teacher to tie a bow in the ribbon of her doll's cushion. The teacher saw that she was interested in how this was done. Sure enough, the girl soon came back and asked the same thing again. This time the teacher made the bow very carefully and slowly, and said this little verse: 'A donkey's ear – and walk round here – go through the big gate – here's the second ear.' After returning twice more with great delight, she learned to tie a bow herself, and started tying them wherever and whenever she could!

We can sum up by saying that the most important thing for preschool children is to learn to play in a way appropriate to their age, and by their own initiative. The concentration developed through play will later prove its worth in the way an adult engages with work. The only difference between 'child's play' and adult work is that the latter must be goal-oriented and integrated into the imperatives of the world. Children's activity, in contrast, comes from inner impulses, from their imagination, with no relation to objective demands of the work itself or of other people. Inner impulses of this kind always invoke pleasure. They engender profound satisfaction, lead to increasing dexterity and the healthy development of intelligence. Herbert Hahn, a teacher at the first Waldorf School in Stuttgart, once said in a talk, 'Wherever powers of play can emerge and unfold, the furrows are being ploughed for a rich harvest later on.'

Teachers in Waldorf kindergartens can accomplish a great deal by introducing real-life activities into their work with children as a stimulus for children's free, imaginative play and active engagement with the world.

Rhythm and Music: Speaking, Singing and Movement Games

Jacqueline Walter-Baumgartner

> In early childhood it is especially important that educational tools such as children's songs make as rhythmic an impression on the senses as possible. The meaning of words is not nearly as important as their beautiful sound. The more that eye and ear are refreshed and enlivened, the better it will be. We should not underestimate the organ-shaping effect of activities such as dancing to musical rhythms.[42]
>
> *Rudolf Steiner*

Cultivation of rhythm and music in finger, action and ring games is a central aspect of early years Steiner-Waldorf education. Fundamental elements of movement, speech and song are intrinsic to such games, which have a firm place in parent and child groups, playgroups, nurseries and kindergartens. These are adapted to the age of the children and reflect the time of day or season of the year. In early childhood there is a greater emphasis on nursery rhymes and lullabies; touching different parts of the body such as hands, feet and head; knee rides; rhymes to soothe and comfort; and simple, rhythmically repeating melodies based on the interval of the fifth. From the ages of two and three, singing and movement games can be done together in a group. These can be developed into ring games for older or mixed age groups and last up to twenty minutes, each one being repeated daily at a set time for at least a week. At kindergarten age, from three to seven, such songs and games become more varied, taking longer and involving more complex movements. Younger children need to experience repetition, and they love it, so the same songs, verses, finger and action games can be repeated for several months.

Below I aim to show how singing and movement games are developed from the gestures of music, rhythm and language, what the nature of their content is, how they address and cultivate children's vital forces and capacities for play and imagination, and how they are embedded in the rhythms of daily life. First, to better understand the importance of rhythm and music in children's lives, let us consider play, movement and imitation and see how they are informed by rhythm, music and language.

The importance of example and imitation in early childhood development

During the first few years of life we can be unselfconsciously active and creatively engaged, both inwardly and outwardly, in a way that will never again be possible. All our first developmental steps, especially standing, walking, moving and speaking, emerge from our capacity for unreflecting imitation of – or we might say active participation in – the examples we experience in our surroundings.

How can we understand this engagement with the world, and self-orientation, through imitation? Young children's direct connection with their surroundings through all their senses, in body, soul and spirit, and the way they find their bearings through these senses, indicates a sleeping or dreamlike awareness of self. In surrender to their surroundings, children learn by experiencing the world around them more vividly than their own body. Environmental impressions work deeply into their physiological processes; for instance, breathing, blood circulation and digestion react sensitively to joyful or sad, nurturing or hectic events in their lives, and inform organic processes of bodily synthesis.[43]

For example, a loud noise, violent expression of anger or the fine aromas of a meal on the plate immediately trigger bodily processes such as rapid pulse, holding of breath, pale complexion or dribbling mouth, besides other reactions such as crying and screaming. The younger children are, the more they respond with their whole body, for instance crawling towards the delicious smells of food.

If a child bangs into something and gets hurt, the tones of a soothing song or a rhythmically spoken verse very quickly help to divert the pain or shock into wondering attention, to calm and harmonise the pulse and breath, and reawaken pleasure. If the song or verse is accompanied by a few rhythmically recurring soothing gestures, such as stroking or cradling – and as long as the adult feels calm – the child's body will grow calm again more quickly.

Young children are not yet centred in themselves but live 'outwardly' among their surroundings. This is reflected in the dream nature of their consciousness and their affinity with magical fairy tales. At birth, children have no experience of earthly realities. During the first seven years the organs prepared in the womb develop and mature, adapting to the world's physical conditions. Children develop to the greatest extent during the first three years, while still wholly given up to their surroundings, and usually before they grasp the meaning of 'I' and use this word to refer to themselves.

Their surroundings, therefore, have the very greatest significance, right into the shaping of bodily organs, and can exert a beneficial effect upon them, above all through the rhythmic regularity of their day, to which the body will orient itself accordingly. Everything of an arrhythmic nature, however, disrupts and prevents organ function from developing in a stable, steady way.

If it is possible, however, to guide and shape young children's basic needs of waking and sleeping, feeding and digesting so that they experience their rhythmic recurrence, they will be all the more content, and soon confirm and consolidate them through their own imitation. The younger children are, the more important it is for them to experience the same actions performed by the same hands, accompanied by the same voice, in gentle tranquillity and attentiveness. The same applies to rhythmic, musical games. It is of the greatest value for children's powers of imitation if they always hear a game or song done in the same way, and if possible by the same adult. Otherwise it is easy for very small children, at least, to feel a sense of disruption. Such regularity and repetition help them to settle trustingly into their surroundings, at the same time confirming their own bodily sense of self.

A loving, affirming education and upbringing nurtures bodily processes. Children sense bodily whether they are loved and accepted, and loving attachment strengthens their immune system, making them feel safe and protected. Lack of love and of interest, irritation, and hectic, rough and neglectful actions endanger this bonding, and impair associated vital forces and powers of bodily synthesis. Ultimately this leads to weakness and lack of protection against negative environmental influences and illnesses.

Adults can exemplify their interest, joy and love through rhythmic and musical games. Being fully present, and connecting actively both with the child and the 'content of play', are key to success, and will elicit happy responses from children.

The importance of play, and the need for archetypal gestures

Until school age, children experience their inner and outer world as one and the same thing. From babyhood onwards, therefore, we see in children's play and imitation not just a reflection of their surroundings but also of their own vital forces, and we can discern how these forces are intimately involved in physical development.

We can use rhythmic words, music and games to draw on children's powers of imitation in a way that nurtures both their physical development and their psychological well-being. Rudolf Steiner discovered that the same powers that are active in developing the body later become available and greatly important for our powers of awareness. To speak metaphorically and generally, we can say that the more children are permitted to surrender to their surroundings in a dreamy, sleeping way, the more their school learning will benefit later from strength, resilience and concentration, and the more they will be able to shape their own lives as adults.

The latest neurophysiological research confirms that all creative free play – which Rudolf Steiner regarded as the most important educational tool – is of key importance for brain development. It is best to play with simple toys that are not too clearly delineated or even just natural materials such as sand, soil, water, shells, stones, leaves, grass, moss, bark, conkers, pine cones, branches, wood, wool etc. These materials provide a range of sensory experiences for children, nurturing their vital forces, because they derive from living nature. This still holds true when they are formed into simple toys, such as cloths or simple human and animal figures. Watching how adults' hands shape and care for things has a creatively formative effect that even works into the infant's brain structure.

This applies likewise to finger and hand games with rhythmic and singing accompaniment: here we use our hands and fingers to playfully characterise and express aspects of the world such as the seasons, the course of the day, natural phenomena etc. Young children immediately understand this language of movement. They have a well-developed inner sense of such things and feel the urge to imitate them. Their developmental path proceeds from grasping literally to grasping inwardly.

Archetypal gestures

What is important is not conceptual understanding of the content of games but rather a rhythmic swinging back and forth between the polarities of archetypal movements. This is what gives young children pleasure and strengthens them. Quite unconsciously and naturally, the very youngest children create rhythmic games, expressing their pleasure, for instance, in hopping movements or by turning their palms alternately up and down. This is often accompanied by rhythmic, melodic calls such as 'ya, ya, yaaah', 'yo-ho! yo-ho!' and 'wah, wah, da, da!' They also love playing with their tongues, creating sounds such as 'lll-lelelelelellll, llooloolloolool, and llliillilliilllll...'[44]

All rhythmically spoken verses and rhymes cause pleasure and hilarity, especially when they are composed only of melodic and rhythmic sounds such as, 'Oolly, woolly, oolly, woolly, oolly, woolly, pack. Oolly, woolly, oolly, woolly, oolly, woolly, snap!'

Healthy movement and play is clearly marked by rhythmically repeating sequences. They tirelessly engage in the ever-recurring archetypal movements of will activity, such as jumping, hopping, swinging, cradling, building, digging, peek-a-boo ('Where's mummy? There!'), filling and emptying, stirring, wrapping and unwrapping objects, covering and uncovering, rolling, throwing, ordering in a row and so on. All these involve motions such as 'back and forth', 'up and down', 'in and out' and 'round and round', which initially occur in a purely functional and imitative way.[45]

For instance, a one-year-old stirs a spoon in a saucepan. If possible, he wants to have the same spoon and pot that his mother is using, because he sees her inner and outer activity as being connected with this. At three or four, his awakening imagination accompanies this initial, functional activity, and now he stirs an imaginary soup with a little stick in a basket. His kindling imagination starts from activity, but is no longer only functional. And in a third developmental phase he engages in his game with inner picturing, now taking on the role of cook and adding a verbal commentary. He does not need new toys all the time, but intentionally chooses the right saucepan or basket 'for the job in hand'. Surprisingly, perhaps, children close to school age still have a particular liking for so-called 'nonsense' rhymes of a rhythmic nature, accompanying them with simple archetypal movements. Sometimes they will invent very funny ones themselves.

These three phases of development (functional, symbolic and role-play), and the need for archetypal movements, are incorporated into the composition of finger and hand games and songs, and ring games. In all of them, movement, speech and song are combined in rhythm and music. And here, too, we find that saying a rhyme only once is no better than never saying it – repetition is all-important.

Until at least the age of six, children have a rhythmic memory bound to location and situation, and, likewise, they unconsciously expect the same thing to happen again when they return to a situation or place. If the habit has been formed, they therefore love saying a grace before a shared meal, and expect to say one.

Rhythmic, archetypal movements, dances and games, like archetypal human activities, embody qualities that are increasingly marginalised today. Arrhythmic and hectic modes of living and working often leave no room for self-directed creative activity, and frequently lead to psychological pressures, loss of inner equilibrium and ultimately to exhaustion. Direct experience of archetypal activities that have a meaningful connection with nature and life itself have largely vanished today. This means that free play, the essence of childhood, and the most vital precondition for subsequent learning, has become something that we and society must consciously nurture.

Every finger rhyme or nursery rhyme is a 'balm' for the child's soul. Free, creative play with simple materials, at a time of diminishing life forces, has become a necessary remedy. Rhythmic finger and action games and songs can therefore be regarded as a kind of gentle medicine, which starts not with children, but with adults, since children learn through imitation. In playing such games regularly, we offer an example worthy of imitation, which enables children to educate themselves.[46]

The effect of hand gestures

Rudolf Steiner's suggestion that early years education should start with the adult's active example and self-education has recently been confirmed by modern brain research, for example, by the renowned neurologist Manfred Spitzer. He has provided neurobiological evidence of the importance of intentional movements for understanding the properties of objects:

> These actions bring about a better embedding of objects in the memory. Acting jointly with others, a good atmosphere in lessons and positive emotions, he says, are especially valuable for learning. Stimulative impulses leave traces in the brain which are then consolidated through repetition and regularity.[47]

The approach of Waldorf education in not only addressing cognitive learning directly, but also (and exclusively in the early years) by practically engaging motor capacities, has likewise proven its scientific validity. Spitzer's thesis that TV and media consumption are damaging to child brain development is also of great significance in relation to rhythm and music in education. There are increasing numbers of modern neuroscientists who now support what numerous educationalists, paediatricians and psychologists have been saying for decades, based on their practical experience: that widespread 'enjoyment' of technical media runs parallel with loss of joyful creativity and imagination in children's play, and has led to the enormous increase in poor concentration, restlessness, anxiety and aggression among children.[48] From the very beginning, Waldorf kindergartens have sought to protect young children from the effect of modern media, and intentionally refrained from employing popular tools such as tape and CD players, radio, (interactive) TV, computers and games consoles. Adults themselves, and their activity and work, are always the focus and example. Rather than passive consumption of image and audio impressions, children experience an adult's active efforts and impulses of will – an active and self-directed ego or 'I'. Honest efforts are what count, not perfection and ready-made provision, and this also enables children to engage in imitation. No loudspeaker can have the same effect.

Our hands make us human. According to research by Frank R. Wilson, human speech and intelligence emerged alongside the development of differentiated hand use.[49] Speech development is very closely related to hand use through crossover in the brain. Fine motor development of finger movements, therefore, at the same time nurtures language articulation. Rudolf Steiner urged teachers to undertake individual studies of the connection between arm or leg movements, and melody, harmony and speech rhythms in young children.

We have many turns of phrase in English that relate to the hand, such as, 'reaching out your hand to someone', 'working hand in hand', 'knowing how to handle something', 'hand on heart', 'having the world at your fingertips', 'taking in hand', 'being in good hands', 'winding someone round your little finger'... and a great deal more. All such phrases can show us that the movements of the hand and fingers inform our thinking and speech. Accompanying hand and finger gestures, rhythmic motions of walking and hopping, and walking on heels or toes all help establish harmonious, fluent and well-structured speech, which in turn creates the basis for the living, logical, ordered, focused activity of inner picturing and thinking.

A hand gesture that corresponds to the content of a verse, song or game is based on careful observation: the way a flower opens, the movement of a wave, the creeping of a snail, the rustling of autumn leaves, the spiralling fall of snow or the floating seeds of a dandelion. What is discovered through observation is then

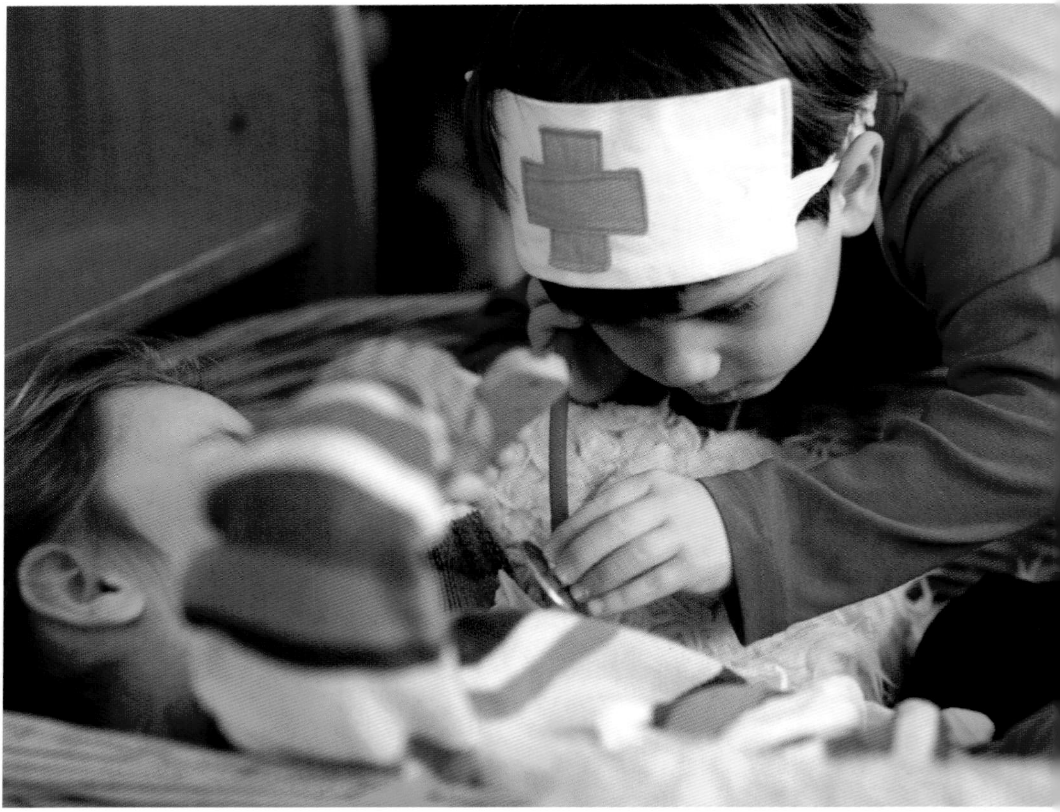

concentrated into its distinctive, unique character and 'translated' into movements of the hand or the whole body. Perceptible reality is embodied artistically – not naturalistically – in the hand, and this is a language young children directly absorb, understand and can themselves enact. The language of hand gestures focuses on process and picture and thus is fully integrated to become bodily knowledge. Archetypal gestures practised at the formative, physical-etheric level, for instance in the peek-a-boo game (open and closed), later metamorphose at the soul-emotional level into a healthy relationship between being together (open) and autonomy (closed), and can give rise to dawning insight at the mental-spiritual level. It is not without reason that children especially love rhythmic and musical games about the sun, whose warming rays awaken the flowers in spring, the animals after their winter sleep and children when the night is over. After all, children themselves are still in a sense buds needing sun-like warmth in order to flourish. Lovingly performed rhythmic games involving physical touch, specifically with the hands or feet, help develop trust and, in the truest sense, enable children to ground themselves on earth.

The effect of speech

At the end of the 1960s, four per cent of children in German-speaking countries were recorded as having initial problems or delay in their speech development. Ten years later this had risen to 25 per cent of three to four-year-old children examined. During the same period the number of illiterate school leavers in the USA was estimated to be seventy million – nearly a third of the population. Today, one in three pre-school children, irrespective of social class or cultural milieu, suffers from speech delays or disorders. In Germany, conferences of speech therapists have confirmed the regrettable finding that conversation between parents and children is restricted to an average of between eight and ten minutes each day, and that children are largely addressed with imperatives.

Such disorders and delays have an effect on children's whole motor and sensorimotor development, and despite therapeutic intervention are discernible well beyond childhood. Lack of conversations in families during the day, and in front of computer or TV, alongside purely intellectual forms of address, mean that children fall silent and are then all the more likely to use their fists to express themselves.

We know that the speech of children born deaf is not well developed – unless measures are taken to counteract this at an early stage – because of their inability to hear things going on around them, and the voices of their parents and siblings. This relates to the phenomena identified above. Speech is part of thinking, and based on differentiated motor development. For this reason, delayed and restricted speech acquisition also impairs emotional and psychological development, since at pre-school age speech is highly emotional. Following the terrible shooting spree by two schoolchildren at Jonesboro in 1998, their supervising psychologist David Grossman expressly stated that, in their exposure to scenes of violence in videos and TV films, they had been subject to the same means and methods the army uses to desensitise soldiers, dismantling their human inhibitions against killing. The more that speech and communication are developed in a complex and differentiated way, the less likely people are to use violence due to a lack of other expressive means.[50]

As early as 1924, Rudolf Steiner suggested that invisible forms arise in the air in front of a speaker's mouth, and vary according to each speech sound. Teacher Johanna Zinke spent years studying this idea, and found ways of rendering such forms visible. High-speed cameras make it possible to record the shapes of speech sounds, and reveal that speech is first and foremost a form-creating movement process. Parallel to this, kinetics research discovered that the whole body performs the subtlest movements accompanying and in response to speech. The researcher William Condon describes this synchronicity of speech and hearing movements as follows: 'Metaphorically speaking, it is as if the whole body of the listener were dancing in a precise and flowing accompaniment to the spoken words.'[51]

Here speech is pure movement or motion, which also unconsciously activates the listener's will and triggers a bodily process of configuring response. The speaker and listener move in a shared stream of singing, speaking and dancing activity.

It is therefore important that the speech forms of rhythmic and musical games focus not on the rational content of words, but on their rhythmic, dynamic and musical qualities. Wilma Ellersiek writes:

> We should attend to the forms of speech sounds, the gestures of words, the rhythmic and musical flow of speech, its melodic sounds, the diversity of sound colours, and the differentiation of dynamics and volume. This kind of speech is close to singing, and by immersing themselves imitatively in the process of configuring speech sound, thus experiencing the gestures and essential qualities of words, children experience archetypal gestures (movement) rather than abstract concepts. For them language is not yet, or not only a descriptive metaphor. In this phenomenon of language as process they can fully incorporate speech into themselves and embody it, thus benefiting comprehensively from its deeply formative entelechy. Here speech and language have a creative function. The child's organism is modelled and shaped by language, right into brain structure, and here lie the foundations for a subsequent creative, imaginative, configuring engagement with language.[52]

The effect of the interval of the fifth

Pentatonic melodies can only move in a swinging motion around a central tone. They float, without a stressed beginning and without tending toward a resolved end. They expand in a

> spiral or in increasing circles and constantly swing back within their own boundaries. They play with tones and are intoning play.[53]
>
> *Fritz Joede*

The mood of the fifth in music, with central tone A, accords with the nature of children up to around the age of eight. Until then they still feel at one with the world: their psyche is immersed in their surroundings, only loosely connected with the body and has not yet fully arrived on earth. For this reason, as described above, healthy children are given up to their surroundings in imitation. The mood of the fifth starts from this experience since it does not relate to a keynote or tonic. The range of tones is optimally balanced around a centre lying in the middle, like a heart. Melodies in the mood of the fifth neither draw us right out into the far breadths of the cosmos, nor give us the grounded experience of being rooted in the material world. By contrast, diatonic melodies have two centres, an opposition or encounter between the keynote and the octave. This introduces the phenomenon of duality and polarity, along with a growing awareness of major and minor keys. The human being's development from 'creature' to free, self-aware 'creator' is reflected in the mood engendered in music in the journey through the seventh, fifth, third to the prime, with the octave as higher polarity.

Music invoking the mood of the fifth, such as lullabies, nursery rhymes, ring-game songs and hand-gesture songs, enable children to open and broaden their souls without losing themselves, to inhabit their bodies happily as a safe, protective house. Simple melodies in this mood can encompass and cradle children who easily get 'out of themselves', or free up those already too solidly in their body. They are capable of soothing the irritants and harmful influences to which children are so often exposed today, and create a sense of tranquillity. Children experience this sense of containment as nurturing, warming protection rather than as restriction. In these tunes children can feel at one with their surroundings, and nestle into them trustingly.

Depending on whether the composition has a rising sequence of tones into the higher fifth, or swings around the central tone, or descends into the lower fifth, we can achieve, respectively: a cheerful, joyous mood; a cradling tonal gesture and bodily exhalation with return to the centre; or the calm sense of soul habitation. It is important for adults to sing gently and not accentuate or dramatise each note too forcefully, but instead create a free, floating sequence of delicate tones.

The effect of rhythm

Our life is embedded in and permeated by countless types of rhythmic sequence. We usually only become aware of their beneficial effect and enlivening power when a rhythm breaks down or peters out, or when a rhythm hardens into static, mechanical, stereotyped routine. A pulse involves the continual recurrence of a similar element – the cycle of the seasons, the orbits of planets, or our heartbeat and breathing – but is never rigid or uniform like a metronome. It flows in a living way, adapting flexibly, sustaining life and health and thus also our life forces:

> The feeling of rhythm in the first seven years is fundamental, based on pulsation. Pulsation is the initial element, the germinal cell of all rhythmic activity[...]. Pulsation has two aspects: it is the polarity between stress and relief, impulse and relaxation (usually denoted as 'pause' or 'rest'), in which something decisive occurs, namely the preparation for another impulse[...]. In the first seven years of life, the blood circulation and breathing only gradually become coordinated. A rhythmic relationship only slowly becomes established and stable.[54]

The healthy relationship of one breath to four pulse beats is a rhythmic measure that only starts to stabilise around the age of eight and later. In early childhood, therefore, strict metronomic pulses, bar lines and note values are too mechanical and rigid, inhibiting, hardening and even disrupting the living current and breathing of organ functions that are still becoming established, along with their formative forces. 'Movement, speech and song should be brought to the child as pulsating activity in support of the building up of the bodily organism and its functions.'[55] It is important to render educational methods suitable for young children by drawing on this living law of rhythm. This involves not only the rhythm and music of songs, verses, games and movement, but also the way in which activities unfold throughout the day. Waldorf kindergartens and early years care ensure that the structure of their day is informed by living, breathing patterns of recurrence, allowing a healthy alternation between 'impetus' and 'rest'. And Waldorf schools then develop such rhythms further in age-appropriate ways.

Practical implementation

It is beyond the scope of this chapter to detail all aspects of methodology in rhythmic, musical, singing, speaking and movement games. I will confine myself instead to a few examples. It is worth emphasising, firstly, that the shortest verse, the simplest song, the tiniest hand gesture game or movement sequence is a total composition that takes artistic account of the following:

1. Breathing alternation between the polarities embodied in archetypal gestures

In other words there is always flux and fluctuation between movements:

- Little/big – sitting as gnomes hunkered down in a root house and rhythmically hammering crystals with fine finger gestures, accompanied by the words of a verse, or melody of a song in the mood of the fifth (or just a few tones). Speech and/or song should correspond harmoniously with the rhythm of movements. Then standing up tall as giants and striding across the land.
- Long/short – leaping like frogs then pulling legs in and squatting. Words correspond to the length of the leap and the shortness of the squatting.
- Back/forth – cradling motions, or forming a leaf swaying back and forth on a branch with hands.
- Open/closed – peek-a-boo game, or a flower that opens in the morning and closes in the evening.
- Forwards/backwards.
- Rising/sinking.
- Loud/soft.
- Quickly/slowly.
- Standing/walking.
- Speaking/singing etc.

Either a speech or music element may predominate, arising either from the content, or to suit the particular group of children. In each instance the most important thing is the rhythmic quality, accompanied by gestures focused on particular actions. It is very effective to incorporate a repeating element – a song or verse.

2. Giving meaningful gestures an artistic form

These may involve activities such as cooking, nursing, sowing and harvesting, craft work and all ways in which people relate meaningfully to their environment; or symbolic representations of the elements – fire, water, air and earth – as well as weather – rain, snow, fog, storm, frost; also qualities and gestures of plants and animals, and the movement of the stars, moon and sun across the heavens. They can include gestures of asking and thanking, of comforting and giving, imaginatively incorporated into little stories. The seasons with their festivals and songs are special high points in the year, in which the activities demonstrated by adults can convey such sentiments as courage, reverence, gratitude, seeking and finding, and so on. Cheerful, festive dances are also integral to this.

Rather than *describing* activities, it is important that adults concentrate on the quality of the gesture itself, embodying the essential nature of what they are representing (the slinking fox, the creeping snail, the flying bird, the scuttling beetle, the floating snowflake, the rattling rain, the leaping flames, the mother cradling a child, the farmer sowing seeds, the gardener watering flowers). Through these gestures, children can immerse themselves in the phenomenon, identifying with or imitating it. Free play in the three developmental stages outlined will also incorporate such qualities. Here, rhythmic and musical games, songs and verses can stimulate and nourish children's play and imaginative engagement.

3. Example and repetition

These are magic words; they enable children to immerse themselves imitatively in activities. Adults, aware that speech sounds, movement and pulsing rhythm help shape and configure children's bodies, should try to speak in a well-articulated, rhythmic and musical way, accompanied by harmonious, buoyant gestures. They should know the games/verses fully so they can always speak the words while carrying out accompanying movements with and in front of children. Children imitate depending on their age, inclination and capacity, but such factors as the weather and physical ailments mean that this can vary a great deal. Here we need tact and sensitivity, calmly continuing with the same finger or hand gesture game at the same time each day over several weeks, and not being too quick to admonish children who don't join in, or asking too much of them. This would merely disrupt the flow of rhythm and music. It is vital to give children time:

> Children more oriented to 'perception' will remain longer in wondering observation, and only gradually find their way into activity. Children who are more 'motor' oriented, on the other hand, will quickly enter into gestures and movements, only later joining in with words and music. The more 'tactile' children take great pleasure in all physical touch, and will gladly do stroking, clapping, tapping and finger interlacing gestures. The 'intellectual' children find it hard to join in and identify with the figures in the game. They will remain observers to begin with, and perhaps offer precocious commentaries. The 'chaotic' children find it difficult to bring their unbridled will into an ordered gesture, and will often initially fail to join in. The 'oversensitive' or 'overwrought' children will turn away because they are too easily overwhelmed. The 'disengaged' children will refuse to join in because they can only be reached through small steps.[56]

If we keep repeating a verse, song or game often enough, all children will eventually join in with words and music, and happily perform the gestures. The more assured and cheerful we adults are in our activity, the more worthy of imitation we will be. Children who find it difficult to participate in the kindergarten or playgroup setting will often do the games themselves at home in quiet moments. The ideal of non-intervention should of course not be confused with denying children our inner engagement and interested, loving observation. A cheerfully spoken phrase, such as, 'First coat, then shoes, then hat – and now we can go out!' will be more encouraging and effective than a hurried or annoyed phrase, such as, 'Now go and get your coat on!' The guiding principle is always to act by example and accompany children's actions, so they are safely encompassed in our care.

In pre-school Waldorf education, we seek to nourish children with rhythm, music and movement games. To extend this metaphor, we try only to use the best 'ingredients': lively speech, meaningful gestures and a nurturing, safely encompassing melodic quality in the mood of the fifth. These games are full of joyful stimulus for play. They kindle the imagination and are imbued with a pulsing rhythm. Leaving children free to imitate in their own good time, adults are wholeheartedly involved in each game, focusing on its archetypal gestures and world of musical sounds with a sense of 'serious cheerfulness'. In this way finger games and ring games nurture children and their healthy development.

Pre-School Eurythmy

Elisabeth Göbel

Rudolf Steiner initiated the movement art of eurythmy in 1912, a few years before he launched Steiner-Waldorf education. Eurythmy enables us to make laws at work in the human form and in our environment visible, and to bring temporal, developmental qualities within us to life. Such laws are drawn both from the formative and structuring powers in the world and from those at work within us, and are available to the artist's shaping will in the same way that every artistic discipline works within its own laws. In attending to movements that correspond to dark and light, that convey the qualities of air, water and not least solid earth, we experience nature around and also within us. The psyche and the mind are likewise informed by light and dark, by fleeting and flowing qualities, as well as by elements of solidity and stability. All such qualities are combined in a rhythmic stream permeating both nature and human beings. Today there is a danger that this rhythmic flux is destabilised in our lives, leading to disruption and even to disease. We scarcely know any longer how to respond naturally and harmoniously to our surroundings, except through conscious effort. Educational eurythmy seeks to aid this harmonisation. Rudolf Steiner developed it at a time when civilisation was beginning to alienate us increasingly from ourselves and our natural environment.

Young children come to know the world by giving themselves up to it entirely in movement. On a walk, for instance, a child will often run three times the length of the route the adult is taking, or delay the intended destination of the walk by balancing on walls or climbing fences. Play at home, too, does not serve any external goal. Instead, children, new to the world, want to engage with and respond to their surroundings, and appropriate them through movement and activity. Eurythmy seeks to meet this need in a varied and focused way, during a weekly session of just half an hour or so. How can we do this?

Eurythmy allows, firstly, children's *capacity for immersion* in the world's diverse phenomena to come to full expression. The eurythmist makes gestures that invite imitation, just as a teacher will sing words and music that children join in with. Secondly, *rhythm* pulses and breathes through each session in all kinds of ways to refresh, enliven and build up children's life forces. Thirdly, eurythmy nurtures children's *joy in their own bodily form* and in their *existence in the world*, conveying a sense of how they are connected or united with things around them. Fourthly, eurythmy supports *speech development* by affirming the whole body experience that sustains it, invoking the diverse movements of speech, which are echoes of movements and formative powers that penetrate and give impetus to the world. Eurythmy translates these universal or archetypal movements into human movement. And fifthly, we can speak of the development of an unconscious *sense of geometry*, which enables children to experience their bodily orientation both in their own form and in the straight lines or circles they move in space. Likewise, a well-prepared session, with rhythmic elements based upon numerical qualities and proportions, can strengthen the natural *mathematical sense* innate in each person.

Below I will describe these aspects in more detail, ending with a discussion of ways that eurythmy sessions comprehensively *nurture the senses*. (Here of course the senses of taste, smell and warmth are not directly invoked but are translated, as it were, into mood or atmospheric qualities.) Besides the five or seven senses traditionally cited, I will discuss others, such as the sense of language and of the thoughts of another person, and above all perception of others in general. All sensory impressions in children – and the younger the child the more pronounced this is – seem to be experienced as immersion and union with what is perceived, far more than in adults, who tend to observe by distancing themselves from things.

To sum up, we can say that children's natural immersion in their surroundings can give rise through eurythmy to a joyful harmony of movements and an unconscious *social dynamic* in space. Taking all this into account, we can see eurythmy sessions as a versatile, child-friendly mode of pre-school education, which does not impose anything on children, but strengthens available capacities and experiential qualities, preparing a healthy foundation for subsequent school learning. Each eurythmist will freely engage with these elements in their own way; a eurythmy session is a kind of artwork itself, which can only emerge from the eurythmist's individual approach and unique experience. Accounts given below, therefore, are intended only as illustrative examples.

A eurythmy session in kindergarten

In full devotion we greet the sun, the clouds, the trees, the earth and – if this fits with the season – the dandelion! 'Good morning, dear sun...' Yes, children are on an equal, friendly footing with the sun. Adults can only move in true accord with such a greeting by identifying fully with children's intimate relationship with their surroundings. Inwardly adults enter the children's stance and sensibility, which allows them to create forms of movement that invoke an authentic and all-permeating sunny feeling. Arms form the round sound of 'O' then shine out into the wide world in the quality of 'Ah'. Children joyfully slip into this experience, giving rise to a mutual experience of 'reciprocal imitation'. Each child is like a small sun, and altogether we are a large encompassing sun. Likewise we become the watery and airy clouds floating across the heavens, lifting our arms upwards and above us in swelling and lifting 'L' and 'V' sounds. The forms of trees are more solid and substantial; their boughs seem to enclose and safeguard us in the character of 'B'. The earth itself we experience as still more solid and stable. We lovingly greet the ground in the rolling consolidation of 'R' followed by the definite 'D' beneath our feet. Our greeting pursues a descending path from light into increasing solidity, echoing the sense of our form from above downwards. And what joy then to discover the dandelion that has just opened its flower, and shines up to us like a tiny sun below on the earth – with which our small hands and all their fingers shine out in radiant accord.

The whole process is borne on rhythmic speech, so we are all permeated by a configuring and musical pulse. In movement, the archetypal element in which young children live, we come to awareness of ourselves and at the same time meet the world by responding intimately to our surroundings. In eurythmy the breathing relationship between ourselves and the world, which we experience in daily life, is deepened and intensified. As well as our natural breathing pattern, our psyche is continually in flux between attending to ourselves and our surroundings, in a continually recurring motion, which moves sometimes more slowly and sometimes more rapidly. How pleased children are to cower together when the words of a verse speak of rain or a storm outside; and how gladly they stretch out their arms again when the sun comes out. The breathing connection between 'me' and 'the world' is continually invoked: whether by sleeping birds in a nest who repeatedly awaken and fly out into the world, then return to the nest again, or by a little mouse hiding in her hole in the cellar who smells a tasty piece of bacon, slips out and – when the cat appears – scurries back into her hole. This kind of archetypal movement is fundamental to human nature, and when its polarities are not in balance we can fall ill, in extreme cases. Children can, for example, be too inwardly 'stuck' and immobile or, alternatively, too 'out of themselves'. Eurythmy can balance any tendencies in one direction or the other in a healing, communal breathing process.

Experiencing the seasons

Children's need to respond to and resonate with everything that surrounds them can be especially nurtured in eurythmy by invoking the breathing rhythms of the seasonal cycle. In spring we experience growth as we lift and flower with the plants, slip out of eggs with nestlings and practise flying. By summer we can fly very well. And when little goats frisk about in the meadow, when fish weave and swim about with water fairies in the stream, when butterflies and bees flutter and hum in the air, then – being all of these things ourselves – we feel at one with the life of nature. In summer the quality of out-breath predominates, even though we must occasionally return to rest in a nest, stable or tree. Then in autumn and winter, in-breath comes into its own, a sense of returning to ourselves. Now we need new shoes and a warm coat. We go to see the cobbler in his dark cellar workshop and focus intently on learning to stitch shoes, teaching small, round fingers to be skilful. When we have made a pair of shoes, we notice – amazing! – that we can first stamp hard or hop in them, but then can creep so quietly that no one can hear us! With great pleasure we learn to look after ourselves. At the tailor's we measure, cut cloth and try to make sure that the coat will fit. We sew a hood for our head then the rest of the coat, 'button by button from top to bottom/and two big pockets to keep hands warm'. This activity focuses entirely on ourselves. In winter, with the gnomes, we make golden plates to take as gifts to the baby Jesus. Snow stars fall from the sky and everything glitters with inner joy. Then in January, a little verse tells us that, 'Even though it's very cold, let's venture out into the wood!' So now we stamp and clap our way with great energy into the New Year. And slowly, towards spring, we start to emerge gladly into the world again. Of course these activities must be adapted to the seasons of the local environment.

In eurythmy sessions there is a continual alternation between gentle and energetic, slow and fast, and evenly streaming movements. Musical tones can accompany and enhance the rhythm of verses: harp or lyre tones are well suited to flying and swimming movements, glockenspiel to leaping and jumping, triangle or tambourine for hammering and tapping. The younger the children, the more suitable are ever-repeating refrains, which give them a sense of security and allow them to keep returning, between onward movements, to the same gestures. Such repetition has a deepening and refreshing effect on them. For the same reason, repeated sequences remain important for older children when portraying short stories or fairy tales. The child's whole body is imbued repeatedly with rhythmic and musical elements, making it supple and dexterous.

Being at home in the body

All this creates the foundations for children to feel at home in their bodies. Immediately after greeting our surroundings it is good to build ourselves a little house, letting four walls grow around us by placing 'stone on stone' with our fists. We look out of the windows on all sides and warmly greet the other children, at last jumping merrily out of the door, then back in, then back out again. 'There we are! Yes, there we are!' call the children cheerfully, leaping into the air, arms stretching up… and then, whoosh, back again into the little house to squat, hidden by their own arms. We do this at least three times in succession.

In this example, the contrast between stretching and contracting embodied in these movements gives children a sense of their inner orientation. Moving straight lines in space and then circular ones creates an unconscious sense of geometry. The interplay of different rhythms based on underlying numerical proportions strengthens the children's bodily sense of mathematical relationships. In subsequent school eurythmy, these aspects are systematically developed alongside geometrical forms in space.

Eurythmy and speech development

We can discern how eurythmy intensifies our sense of language and thus can help support speech development by realising, for instance, that we would never perform hard or angular movements to accompany words such as 'Sighing breezes wafting softly'. The arm movements for the 'S' sound are airy, light and curve swiftly through space. By contrast, in something like, 'Hack, hack, the rocks we crack', angles and hard edges of the 'K' sound seem fully appropriate, and as we move, our steps will adapt to this quality. When we listen to another person talking, the movements of speech very faintly reverberate in us, in our speech organs but also reaching beyond them to other parts of the body. Eurythmy takes these subtle speech movements and broadens them to encompass the whole body, so that it 'speaks' in corresponding gestures. The gestures of sounds become eurythmy's configuring element. We can sense here how speech sounds make formative powers audible, and that these same powers originally formed our body and now in turn become visible through it. Thus we can almost see the children's little bones clattering and ringing, as gnomes in a story drag their treasures of crystals and stones through cracks in the rock:

Clumping, clattering comes the gnome
Jerking his heavy sack, dragging it home.

The dialogue here is with the solid nature of the mineral world. A dialogue with watery elements has a completely different feel, as in this little poem about a spring:

Out of darkness into light
I bring lovely water bright.
From the earth I bubble and sing,
'Look at me: I am the spring!'

The movements, accordingly, will be flowing, lifting, swelling ones, like a slowly bubbling spring, whose living flow the children embody in space. Vowels have a different quality again, being more intimately expressive of our feelings. We say 'ah' to express joyful wonder, or 'oo' if we're afraid or feel cold. These examples suffice, hopefully, to show how eurythmy can help develop a sense of language qualities, either in a group or one-to-one. In this way formative developmental processes in pre-school children are supported, without any inappropriate recourse to intellectual concepts that would diminish the power and effect of these movements.

Eurythmy and the senses

While young children dwell in 'mythic consciousness' their sense perceptions are different from those of adults. The self-focused *sense of touch* serves, as described for instance in the 'wall-building' game, to engender an experience of the process of growing taller. With the shoes, which first stamp and then creep quietly, children are not focusing on the experience of soles touching the ground, but of the shoes' magic properties. What invokes inner pictures in young children is something we might call a 'metaphysical touching'.

The *sense of life* is very important for young children. Eurythmy gestures will only be effective if children are feeling well. The eurythmist's lively enthusiasm encourages children to feel lively and healthy too. A loving environment enables children's organs to flourish, and opens them up in wholehearted engagement with the world around them.

We use the *sense of movement* to understand our own movements, as well as perceiving external movements and forms. This is cultivated especially in eurythmy, which imbues everything that we see and hear, and recognise as language. This sense of movement provides the foundation for responding intimately to the world, not merely physically but also in soul and spirit, in real interplay. This is why it is so important to practise eurythmy today: inner and outer immobility and inflexibility are the last thing we want for our children, but that is precisely what they are being pre-programmed for through television and media consumption.

The *sense of balance* is activated in very lively, happy fashion when we trot or gallop on imaginary horses as valiant riders, but at any moment can pull up our steed and halt him, before riding on or urging him into a daring leap. Here great self-mastery is needed, leading to wonderful strengthening of our own balance.

As stated earlier, the *senses of taste, smell and warmth* only appear in a figurative sense in eurythmy. The power of imagination with which children picture, say, a little mouse smelling something tasty, is very intense, and can spread a current of well-being through them. The sense of warmth they experience in safety and security is vital.

The *sense of sight* is one of the most important gateways through which we engage with the world. Here we need to realise that young children see things more vividly and vibrantly than we do. They see and experience the secret of a dark wood or the enchantment of a flower-strewn clearing, where the Easter hare and the flower elves live. These qualities can be rendered visible for children through eurythmy, who do not see things externally but have a totality of perception. This applies likewise to perception of their key attachment figure, from whom they imitate certain gestural qualities. As this attachment figure, we can get a strong sense of being 'seen' in our totality, and being accompanied by children's almost simultaneous responses and movements.

Since young children cannot yet separate themselves from impressions – the younger the less so – the *sense of hearing* has a far more comprehensive effect on them than it does on adults. This is why, in eurythmy, musical instruments are carefully chosen, for the range of tones should neither overstretch young children's receptivity nor constrict it through semitones or dissonances. Both will overburden young children's ears. We may be able to sense the impact thundering traffic noise or harsh electronic music has on them. And for this reason, in the protected space of kindergarten, we accentuate harmonious sound qualities all the more.

Hearing is the sensory gateway to another, distinct sense: that of *speech perception*. Besides the content of meaning and the melodic nature of speech, children also notice whether the words spoken bear a creative stimulus and are authentic and truthful. They observe holistically whether a person's language is informed by a rich inner world and clear thinking; perceiving, in other words, the whole nature of the person they hear speaking. They drink the person in, entirely and bodily, and this makes deep impressions on them.

As a eurythmist, therefore, we can feel a special sense of responsibility, as we are working with the creative powers of language, striving for clarity in the thoughts we enact, and revealing our intrinsic being to children through movement. Thus children perceive us through a unity of the three higher senses – speech perception, the sense of another's thoughts and the sense of another's intrinsic being or 'I'. In kindergarten eurythmy sessions, children receive a deep foundation that will later feed into their conscious development as adults.

In decades of work as a eurythmist in kindergartens I have often felt that, when arriving there from my daily life or from school, the crowd of little ones coming towards me bring a 'little piece of heaven' with them, a gift of trust that shines from their eyes. Eurythmy can intensify this heavenly experience, allowing it full scope. Children feel at home in it, and for a while can re-immerse themselves in their 'original home'. One can sense that this feeling will strengthen them in their future lives, on their individual paths and in all social contexts, living in them as a profound, unconscious experience. We do not need to be great philosophers to notice, today, the fundamental importance of such childhood experiences for all domains of life, and how this will stand children in good stead when it comes to discovering real values to live by.

Balancing the Effects of Media

Andreas Neider

A balanced approach to media

Before examining the question of how to handle the world of media during the first seven years of childhood, I would like to define the principle of 'media balance'. Modern, media-based educational principles speak of 'media competency', meaning the capacity to handle media of all kinds. No further distinction is made between different forms of media. The concept of media balance, which I place alongside this, means that all involvement with media requires a balancing activity. Why do I suggest this?

As we will see below, each form of media primarily addresses a specific area of human experience. Basically, we can distinguish three (connected) realms of the human psyche:

- Picturing and thinking
- Sensing and feeling
- Will and action

Pre-school children can engage actively in each of these three domains. Or a specific form of media can substitute their own activity, which I will elaborate on below.

An overview of the different media

In the beginning was the book

A survey of media brings us firstly to books – picture books for young children and fiction for children, including reading books at school. Text and books were the first form of media in our cultural history, and for a long time the primary one. They were followed eventually by the media of film and television.

Like a book, the medium of television relates stories and presents images, with the key difference that screen images come towards children from without and do not have to created by them. Both media, books and television, strongly address children's *picturing capacity* and the *neurosensory realm*. The vital difference is that activity is required in comprehending books, whereas children remain passive when watching television. In the first seven years, children may well not yet be reading themselves, but being read to. We will go on to examine what this means for their own subsequent reading.

Audio at the touch of a switch

Going a step further we meet the level of *feelings*. Here we find the most widespread medium of all in terms of children's use of media: the MP3 player or CD player for listening to audiobooks and music. This medium is roughly as old as the image media of television or cinema. Today, ubiquitous equipment gives access to audio content round the clock and everywhere you go, from the radio alarm to the bedtime lullaby.

When listening to music, passive consumption can be counteracted by an active element, when children themselves make music, play an instrument or join an early years music or singing group. Other artistic activities, such as painting – which also relates to the domain of feeling – can also supplement musical games and activities.

Virtual and real play

A third medium, more addressed to the *will*, is that of computer games either on a PC, a games console or a cellphone. This later development in the media landscape appears to overcome the passive nature of media consumption, for the player is actively involved in games. And yet this is not entirely so, for passivity still lurks here in the form of physical inactivity. It is in free play that children can really engage their will and associated feelings.

The principle of media balance

- Media balance, therefore, means counteracting every kind of passive media consumption with a balancing activity. But in pre-school years specifically, it is important to ensure that we establish as much autonomous activity as possible in all three realms of the psyche, for this will guard against the effects of media consumption later on. If we consider this in relation to business accounts, we can say that the more income I have earned, the more expenditure I can subsequently make. Periods of passive media consumption must always be measured against others during which children have engaged in active pursuits. Children who have primarily been active in the first seven years will later be less inclined to need so much passive media consumption, as they have learned to be active themselves!

In relation to media education, as in other areas, the first years of life are the most important. It is enormously difficult to establish the balance referred to here if children have been surrounded by electronic media from a young age. Media balance at pre-school age can be regarded as completely avoiding the media that will increasingly play a part from school age onwards, focusing on children's own activity to counteract the later effect of media.

Domain of the psyche	*Passive Media*	*Activities*
Picturing, thinking	Film, television	Being read to, reading
Feeling, emotions	MP3 player	Making music
Will, social relationships	Computer games, internet, cellphones	Play

Media balance for childhood

Domain of the psyche	*Passive Media*	*Activities*
Picturing, thinking	Television	Finger games, fairy tales, being read to
Feeling, emotions	CD player	Singing, nursery rhymes, children's songs, musical games, making music
Will, social relationships	Computer games, internet	Free play

Media balance at pre-school age.

We will outline activities in childhood that correspond to and counterbalance each form of media, with the proviso that at pre-school age such media should figure as little as possible and preferably not at all.

First domain: speech and language

A culture of reading aloud can initially be established through oral narratives involving short poems, rhymes and finger games rather than longer or more complex texts.[57] Playful engagement with language and movement is an ideal mode of communication between young children and adults. If children have the attention span to follow short stories, picture books can be used and stories told, until they begin to want to read themselves.

The following age indications are only a rule of thumb and will vary with each child:

- Ages 1 to 3: verses, rhymes and finger games – playful engagement with language.
- Ages 3 to 5: picture books, short fairy tales and stories – telling or reading aloud.
- Ages 5 to 6: children's books and Grimm's fairy tales – reading aloud.
- Ages 6 to 7: children's books – starting school, begin to read by themselves.

Some parents are uncertain when they should tell their children fairy tales, or whether they should do so at all. This is because many of these tales contain images that seem cruel or alarming to adults. Yet children's world of imagination is different from that of adults. In her very readable book, *Die Märchenleiter* (*The Fairy Tale Ladder*), Arnica Esterl describes the special nature of the language in fairy tales. She compares the simple prose of an ordinary narrative (first passage below) with that of a simple fairy tale (second passage):

> When I was young we didn't have much to eat. My mother just used to put bread and dripping in my hand and send me out to the forest, telling me to play. My friend Jan ran about in the forest; he had just discovered a rabbit's hole. So we found long sticks, and poked holes in the ground everywhere to try to annoy the rabbits and make them come out.

> Once upon a time there was a poor, kind-hearted girl who lived alone with her mother, with little enough to eat. One

> day the child went out into the forest and met an old woman there who already knew of her sorrows, and gave her a little pot to which she should speak the words, 'Cook, little pot, cook.' Then it cooked good, sweet porridge. And when she said, 'Stop, little pot, stop,' it stopped cooking again.[58]

If you read both passages aloud you will have an immediate sense of the difference. The language of the fairy tale conveys a very particular mood that leads children into their own inner world – the fairy tale world – and comes to expression in inner images rather than realistic facts. The more neutral narrative tone of the prose piece, by contrast, acquaints children more with the mundane, everyday world. Both are important, and neither form can be substituted for the other.

No fear of late development

There are no absolute age norms, since each child develops in an individual way. There is no need to feel anxious if a developmental phase takes longer or is delayed – for instance, if children do not immediately start reading books by themselves when they reach school age. The important thing is that children's engagement with literature and language, and the thinking and picturing capacities and powers of imagination stimulated by it, is not to be neglected in favour of other media such as CDs and audiobooks. Children learn from the adult's example. If this is lacking, having been replaced by electronic media, the processes of speech and language development described here cannot really come into their own.

On the other hand, we should take care that learning to read does not start before six or so; children's powers of thinking are not mature enough to support the efforts needed in learning to read until this age. We should certainly avoid pressurising young children into reading or introducing it at pre-school age.

We can start introducing children to books from a young age by saying traditional nursery rhymes aloud, then by telling short stories or reading to them aloud,[59] before moving on to the world of fairy tales collected by Grimm and others. Without this culture of storytelling or reading aloud, children will later find it difficult to relate to or engage with books. If, on the other hand, they have grown used to being read to, they will later be able to continue the process of actively creating inner images when they read books themselves. This process also facilitates the development of personal strengths and the capacity for judgement: if we can meet whatever we experience with strong powers of visualisation, it strengthens our own sense of self and orientation in the world. Instead of feeling like puppets manipulated by the strings of pre-packaged impressions, young people can develop autonomous, alert and critical awareness.

Audiobooks are no substitute

Fairy-tale CDs and downloads are simply no substitute for an adult reading a story aloud or telling it. Quite apart from the fact that many such recordings are distorted by unnatural voices, unsuitable musical backing etc., these 'virtual readers' cannot replace an actual adult since they exclude any chance of conversation and question-and-answer exchanges. Children sit there mutely. They may, however, listen to a tape so often that they can later recite it.

A father told me that his children, who lived with their mother from whom he was divorced, continually listened to story CDs and could regurgitate their content. He was saddened that his children took their lead from a machine rather than from live stories and songs. Apart from the fact that they reproduced the recordings in an identical and lifeless way each time, he regretted that his children's gifts for retelling a story were being 'taught' by a mechanical object rather than by their mother.

Reading as key skill

There is a clear difference between reading and all other media. Whereas children are stimulated to form their own inner pictures and judgments by being read to and later when they read themselves, all visual media relieves them of this active process by supplying ready-made images. The more dependent children are on visual media, the more inwardly passive they will become, the more their own powers of judgement will wane and the more, in turn, the inner vacuum arising in consequence will seek to be filled by externally provided images. Ultimately a kind of addiction is created. While reading strengthens autonomous capacity for judgement, consumption of image media tends to weaken it. But if, from school age onwards, children become proficient in reading, they will be less in thrall to all other media that does not encroach so radically on their autonomy. They may well absorb such media, but it will not so easily gain dominance over them.

We see, therefore, that reading is a key skill in a world dominated by image media. Someone who reads a lot will more easily retain a critical stance towards other media, through being better able to select and evaluate things that are personally relevant. The word 'literacy' in English, to describe competency in reading and language, offers an interesting insight into the wider cultural value of this skill.

Second domain: music

Literacy development, therefore, starts in early childhood with rhymes and finger games. What listening and reading are in the domain of language, singing is in the musical domain. Today, sadly, many mothers and fathers no longer know and sing lullabies and nursery rhymes as a matter of course. The well-known conductor Nicolaus Harnoncourt said:

> If children can't sing, I'd say the parents are to blame, since they haven't sung with their children. Almost everyone can sing. You have to locate the notes, and this is no problem if you have done it from a young age. An unmusical person is one who had the misfortune to have no contact with music when young. There is global consensus that every person has the right to learn to be numerate and literate. And likewise every person should learn to sing. Today, sadly, there is no longer a general view that schools also have a responsibility to develop artistic potential. In former times every primary school teacher could play the piano or the violin.[60]

In my view, it is of primary importance that parents engage with their children's musical education. Why not join a choir or pursue musical activities alongside other pregnancy exercises today regarded as normal preparation for birth? There is really no better medium than music for the emotional relationship between children and parents. Even if you think you can't sing well or 'properly', your children will still benefit more from the human intimacy of your singing than they will from the best CD of children's songs.

Many books contain ideas and stimulus for singing with young children.[61] Nursery rhymes and lullabies are followed by songs that children can easily join in with. You can also introduce first musical instruments (glockenspiel or lyre) that help children explore the realm of musical tones. And rhythmic movements such as clapping and walking in a ring can also play a part. The well-known music teacher Dorothée Kreusch-Jacob writes on this theme:[62]

> Children sing better and more happily if they don't have to sit still as they do so[...]. We can see this interplay of body and voice most clearly in the youngest ones. Singing and beating a rhythm have little effect if their whole body cannot join in.

Not all parents, of course, will feel confident enough to sing or play music with their children. There are, however, plenty of pre-school music and singing groups run by trained music teachers, outside of a kindergarten context.

A whole range of instruments has been developed for pre-school children. Their very delicate sounds are particularly suited for schooling young children's hearing and musical sensitivity. For instance, music teacher Juergen Knothe writes about the pentatonic lyre:[63]

> The pentatonic lyre is a stringed instrument with open sound box, usually made of ash and developed for kindergarten and pre-school. The seven strings of this relatively small instrument are stretched across an open frame and a sounding board, and tuned pentatonically, therefore without major-minor orientation. A magical, floating sound arises by gently stroking the strings. The lyre can be used for movement games, improvisations and simple melodies in groups or with individual children.[64]

Although parents want to nurture and support children individually at home, many are wary of embarking with their children on musical explorations. Below are a few suggestions for approaching new listening experiences.

New sound landscapes

The first step is to discover as many noises as possible in children's immediate surroundings. To do so, we can set off on a little journey through the various rooms of our home, discovering, say, the murmuring of water in the pipes, the noise of kitchen appliances, of zip fasteners, and a great many other sounds. Then we can continue our explorations outside, where we may first hear the noises of machines such as cars, buses, but also other children laughing, or a dog barking. Walking further in a natural environment we might hear wind in the trees, the noise of our feet through fallen leaves, twigs cracking underfoot or a brook babbling by the path. Children can describe what they hear: does it sound soft or loud, high or low, happy or sad?

Little exercises like this can give children and adults new experiences, and through them a deeper level of connection. In the process adults can learn which sounds enhance appeal to them and their children, and which do not.

Third domain: play

As in the two areas of 'media balance' we have described – literacy and music – it is never too soon to engage in play. The solid foundations for life that children establish in play contribute decisively to their development.

Psychotherapist Eckehard Schiffer repeatedly draws attention to this in his writings:

> Through play we come to key insights that we can never approach by engaging with facts and formal logical structures – in school lessons for instance. Of primary importance here is the insight into what does us, and others, good. And play – understood here as an archetypal form of creative activity – is involved whenever we are innovative and creative[...]. Here we can recall the world of Huckleberry Finn, Pippi Longstocking and Momo. Such play also involves being able to stop and quietly observe things. It means shaping and perceiving the world, and allowing invisible things to become visible, as if through the eyes of the Little Prince. No doubt we idealise childhood experiences, but they do nevertheless remind us of our own potential. Primal powers are at work in these worlds – a love of discovery and activity, sensory experience and the desire

> to make things happen; a love of shaping things actively rather than just suffering them passively.[65]

These words say everything that needs to be said in relation to media balance. Schiffer goes on to highlight that in his therapeutic work almost all treatment of psychosomatic disorders starts from these primal powers of children's play. He once told me, 'If my patients had played more in childhood, we wouldn't have to make up this lost ground later in our clinic.' This, too, says a great deal about the character and importance of play.

Generally, play and its establishment in the early years depend on:

- Giving children as much scope as possible for play.
- Not giving them pre-determined frameworks or materials for their play.
- Giving them opportunities for play in which they can shape and create things themselves.

The relevant literature offers more food for thought on this.[66]

Media in the first seven years?

To sum up, it is best to expose children to as little media as possible before the age of seven; they will by nature always feel most at home on the active side of media balance if not prematurely exposed to passive media consumption. The activities described here can help counteract subsequent media consumption – which is inevitable and ought not to be demonised – by establishing a healthy range of balance and autonomous, creative engagement to begin with. Returning to the metaphor of income and expenditure, we store up an important asset for schoolchildren and adolescents by creating these initial foundations.

Mouse-Clicking Through Childhood?

Peter Lang

Computers and software for two-year-olds are now being sold to parents as educationally valuable. There is talk, also, of equipping kindergartens with computers as part of early years provision. None of these plans question the benefit of engaging with this technology at pre-school stage, let alone consider that it may be harmful to child development. But despite all political – and manufacturer-supported – propaganda, no TV or computer can give children what they need in the first years of life.

Let me be clear that I am not in any way rejecting computer technology in general, which has been an inevitable part of our lives and work for a long time now, and is an extremely helpful and useful tool. It makes a great deal of work much easier and quicker, and gives us access to a wealth of information. Technology has been a firm part of the Steiner-Waldorf school curriculum since its founding in 1919, and pupils in middle and upper school should naturally become acquainted with technological developments and learn to use them.

Children are sensory beings

To understand and engage with the world, however, children need sensory perceptions. They must have direct, first-hand experience of things by touching, holding, smelling, tasting, hearing and seeing them. The path to autonomous insight and understanding leads from grasping literally to grasping metaphorically. The feel of water, the sound of metal or wood, the smell of an apple, the darkening of twilight or the smell of cheesecake are all sensory experiences that 'inform' children's senses.

By contrast, computers only offer a world one step removed – through copies and imitations. Even the best painting or crafts program on a two-dimensional screen, with its virtual paint brush or artificial scissors and mouse click-created movements, does not come anywhere near the learning experience connected with experiencing actual colours and materials. Worse, it deceives children because they cannot yet distinguish between a real and a virtual world. Children absorb everything their senses offer them as reality, and their power of imagination animates. Only when we develop the capacity to think, perceive and judge independently can we clearly distinguish between appearance and reality. Young children cannot yet do this, but are dependent on adults to show them the world as it really is, and not as it appears on the screen. Children have a right to reality.

Children are gifted with imagination

Children's powers of imagination are initially dependent on sensory perceptions and diverse experiences. Then, with its help, children free themselves from the world of purely sensory impressions, releasing their experiences from their original contexts, and allowing something new to emerge through their own active, creative processes. Children create new worlds through the power of imagination every day. They do so in a particularly intense way because they have a deep need and innate capacity to absorb everything with interest and sympathy, connecting, merging and enhancing it.

Children's software, with its predetermined template of possible actions, invariably restricts their imaginative powers, and does not offer any basis for creative and innovative capacities in future years.

Toys that leave free scope for the imagination, and natural materials with their unlimited diversity of shapes and colours, stimulate children's creative faculties far more than the best software. Fairy tales told by an actual person and explorations of the natural world kindle imaginative activity, whereas software permits only the elaboration of a pre-programmed context.

There is now a great deal of evidence from neurobiological research to show that an initial, intense reciprocal engagement with the real world, over many years, is highly significant for healthy and differentiated brain development. The renowned neurobiologist Manfred Spitzer writes, for instance:

> Only by trying to touch water can I learn what its wetness means. At the same time I hear it gurgle or drip, see its waves or currents, perhaps smell the sea or the grass by the riverbank, and thus gain an overall impression which – together with other such experiences – develops within me into a complex and differentiated representation of water. If I do not (yet) have this inner representation I will not be able to understand even the most colourful images or flashy tones issuing from the computer. This is why there is no place whatever for computers in a pre-school child's room, kindergarten or nursery. Even in schools their use should be appraised far more critically than is currently the case in this era of technology euphoria.[67]

Children live in movement

To explore the world you have to set off on a journey. For children this means walking, leaping, climbing, balancing, rope skipping, digging and building sand castles. It also means drawing, painting, modelling and chopping vegetables – activities in which they train their own finger dexterity and develop their fine motor skills. Back in the forties of the last century, the Swiss psychologist Jean

Piaget recognised that children's movement is a key foundation for their cognitive, social and emotional development.[68] He was aware that a failure to develop a sense of balance would have later repercussions on psychological equilibrium. Movement disorders often correlate with delayed speech development. Impairment of sensory development has an impact on cognitive development and learning. A society that does not nurture the sensory development of its young generation will at the same time diminish the scope of its intellectual capacity.

Besides the hands, arms and legs, the human eye is also an organ of movement. When we look at something close up or look away into the distance, our lenses are in continual movement; the pupil expands or contracts in response to light conditions. To observe an object, our eyes move across its outlines and various parts.

Computer work markedly restricts this motion of the eyes. The distance between eye and appliance always remains the same, and the three-dimensional quality of space is cancelled and simplified into two dimensions, while colour qualities are artificial. Children's field of vision, whose scope can normally extend to two hundred degrees, is increasingly narrowed – in the worst case to seventy or eighty degrees. The eyes of children who watch a lot of television or sit at the computer a good deal, lose their mobility over time. These children then find it harder to maintain their balance, to ride a scooter or bicycle say, and are much more likely to have accidents. Early engagement with computers inhibits movement development.

Speech is the cradle of thought

Children learn to speak in a speaking environment, and have an innate impulse to do so. But clearly the opportunities to develop this faculty are considerably diminished today. Over the past 25 years, speech development disorders have increased rapidly. Nearly one in four children aged between three and four shows such impairment. Deficient speech development is in turn associated with psychological problems and an inability to express one's own feelings and convey them to others. Children's psychological breadth and inner experiential capacity are impoverished. Early speech disorders also inhibit the development of thinking faculties.

Children need to learn to think independently in order to understand the world and themselves. They need to connect what they observe and feel with their thoughts to create meaning, distinguishing cause and effect, engaging with ideas and actively reflecting on what they and others think.

Increasing numbers of studies are recognising the connection between speech and thinking disorders on the one hand, and regular use of electronic media on the other.[69] Even TV, where children hear continual speech, does not support speech development. This is because just hearing spoken words is not sufficient. There are two other factors that no television or computer can replace: firstly, the positive social relationship between the speaker and the listener; and secondly, the example the adult sets, which the child actively imitates.

Technology has relieved us of considerable effort: machines do physical labour for us, and computers have found their valued place in our life and work. But such helpful, useful tools are harmful for children. If their lives are governed by mouse clicks, they have ever fewer opportunities to experience their own bodily powers and explore their individual creative capacities. On computers, children's activity is cut down to software size: virtuality instead of reality, and conditioning instead of development.

Life doesn't come at the touch of a button

Life appears to many children to be fully automated, or like a magic trick: you push a button and a machine is set in motion, a light goes on or off, the vacuum cleaner begins working, a car starts.

Children today see ever fewer connected and comprehensible sequences of action, let alone practise and learn to accomplish such actions themselves.

A key educational task, therefore, is to offer them experiences that they can grasp in their entirety, seeing both cause and effect, and themselves learning to act purposefully. On an expedition to a farm, for example, they can see the sacks of grain, smell the corn and feel the grains trickling through their fingers. Their senses are activated. They can buy a small bag of grain from the farmer and take it back to kindergarten. Next day the children grind the corn with a hand mill, which takes strength and persistence. Then they can knead dough, shape bread rolls or loaves, and bake them in the oven. A wonderful smell of baking bread wafts through the kindergarten. The table is laid, a song is sung or a grace spoken: the children thank the sun, the rain, Mother Earth or God who helped the grain to grow. And then they eat the rolls with gusto. Just this one example contains such a wealth of interconnected observations and experiences. All of this – sensory perceptions, inner experiences, children's own activity, social togetherness, the logic implicit in meaningful sequences of activity, and the sense of gratitude – forms a stable foundation upon which school children can subsequently build the connectivity of their thinking and insight.

Computers in kindergarten make no contribution to this. They are a false investment not only in financial terms, but also psychologically and educationally. Young children cannot yet understand how they function or discern any true relationship between cause and effect in their use. They scarcely gain any sense of their own activity from them.

Models of violence

It is, however, not just a matter of the computer per se but also of the content it conveys. The very term 'computer game' is largely misleading, since many such games do not involve playful exploration of reality. They draw on violence as a thrill and provide models of violence – at least indirectly. Studies so far undertaken clearly indicate that media violence has a negative impact on children's behaviour.[70] Levels of aggression rise, and acceptance and normalisation of violence grows. This leads to a creeping process of psychological desensitisation and the suppression of basic human qualities such as sympathy, love, care, concern and the desire to help. Research undertaken at Bochum University also highlights the fact, however, that children growing up in an emotionally protected milieu are less vulnerable to this desensitisation to violence than those who live in emotionally volatile circumstances. Lack of emotional attachment prepares the ground for aggression, and growing aggressiveness drives children and adolescents into an increasing lack of attachment: a vicious circle of violence is set in motion. Even if kindergarten children do not as yet have any access to violent games, the ground is being prepared for this. Children become acquainted with computers, their engagement with it becomes normality, and at some point or other they will gain access to a different kind of content.

A right time for everything…

Computers are now part of everyday reality for many parents. An unholy alliance between the communications industry, government education programmes and modernisation theories is increasingly putting pressure on kindergartens, schools, parents and teachers to submit to these new technological developments. 'We have to prepare our children for the modern world of work', 'We don't want our children to grow up in a world removed from reality' or 'Computers are a fact of life now, so we have to learn how to handle them – and the earlier children learn to do this the easier they'll find it'… Such opinions are commonly expressed by many parents and teachers, who of course want the best for the children in their care.

Yet properly understood, educational responsibility leads to the opposite point of view. As already made clear, it is not a matter of demonising computers, which are very useful tools in the adult world, but of questioning whether they serve the interests of young children, who primarily learn by playing and through their own exploratory activity. They do not desire their work – which is play – to be 'made easier', especially not before they have properly appropriated this important and demanding mode of activity.

Children do not 'get the information they need' at the click of a mouse, for in doing so they learn nothing primary and intrinsic to them. They learn through perceiving, imitating and self-directed, imaginative activity. This increases their 'store of experience' so that they become inwardly and outwardly active, taking hold of the world around them and linking its different aspects in meaningful ways, thus constructing their own, first-hand reality. In this way their thinking is not compelled into abstraction from the outset.

The more purposeful and consistent the actions of exemplary adults, the more children's actions can unfold in a meaningful context. Later, a long time after kindergarten, children's thinking emancipates itself from direct perception and is no longer dependent on the immediate situation and their own actions, but becomes increasingly free.

Children's imagination at kindergarten age is still entirely bound up with play and creative activity engaged with the immediate world around them. At adolescence, and still more so in adulthood, these powers of the imagination can transform into creative powers of thinking, detaching themselves from their original, close involvement in a particular activity. Thus the adult's imagination becomes free for shaping new ideas and challenges.

At pre-school age, children primarily practise their social capacities in group play (which includes learning to resolve social conflicts), celebration of seasonal festivals, shared stories that help orient them, and by gradually taking on small tasks and duties.

Computers make no contribution to these learning experiences, and do not offer what young children need: sensory perception, imagination, movement, conversation and creative thinking. Computers in kindergarten inhibit children's development and rob them of their childhood. The motto 'The earlier the better' is pervasive in our culture. But it is high time to set another against it: 'There is a right time for everything.'

Nutrition in Kindergartens Today

Michael Kassner

The current situation

Rapid and diverse changes in society mean that kindergarten children's requirements are continually changing too. Young, newly trained kindergarten teachers likewise bring with them different insights and skills. In the realm of nutrition, specifically, these upheavals mean new challenges in daily kindergarten life.

- Children bring different habits with them from home.
- They have clearly varying preferences, which develop at a considerably younger age.
- They are quick to voice or demonstrate their inclinations or refusal.
- Appetite, thirst and feelings of hunger often seem to be overlaid by other moods.
- Sometimes children only want foods they are familiar with and do not tolerate change.
- They show signs of metabolic weakness that cannot be ignored.
- They increasingly suffer from diseases such as neurodermitis, allergies or a disposition to obesity.

Young teachers, also, are no longer necessarily experienced in preparing food.

- Their knowledge of nutrition is often one-sided, incomplete or tinged by their own personal predilections.
- They haven't received any training in this field, and none is offered.
- They may have been influenced by kindergarten parents with particular views about nutrition.
- They are fully preoccupied with the extensive demands of their work as kindergarten teachers, and therefore have little time or energy to study a new field.

The following suggestions and stimulus for a modern approach to nutrition in Steiner-Waldorf kindergartens is set against this – no doubt incomplete – background, as a guideline that may need modifying in relation to individual children or particular circumstances. It should also be noted that we are chiefly considering nutrition here, rather than its place in the social dynamic of the kindergarten group, which would require additional reflections.

An approach to nutrition oriented to healthy child development should not lay down prescriptive schemas or exclude certain foods, but aim to offer a foundation, based on deep understanding of the human being and child development, which can help people make their own free choices.

Nutrition and joy in life

In profound wisdom, nature provides an ideal food – breastmilk – for the first months of human life. It is normally only at weaning that the question of suitable food for children arises. And then the question can become a minefield, as such a wide range of food is available; this can be problematic not just for the parents but also for children.

Every new food is a challenge for the digestive system, requiring it to form appropriate digestive powers and juices. The metabolic organs are only germinally developed to begin with and need around seven years of 'schooling' to unfold their full functionality and resilience. This presents parents with a big responsibility for a long period of time. While immune function matures at around three months – nine months in the womb and three months outside, making a full year before individual immune defence begins – at least seven years are needed for the basic development of metabolic organs.

Below, in examining more closely the period from three (start of kindergarten) up to school age, we find three aspects of nutrition to consider:

- How can we help the digestive organs to develop healthily?
- How can we nurture gratitude towards the human, animal and plant realms, and towards heaven and earth, in the way we engage with food?
- How does our own example, also at the table, introduce children to a sense of social community?

Children approach the world with 'playful seriousness' and we can tackle these challenges in the same way. At pre-school age children are more open to new things than they will ever be again, continually balancing between habit – security based on experience – and inquisitiveness. They usually have a sound instinct for what they can cope with, for this knowledge draws directly on their metabolic organs rather than on their minds and intellect. Deep within them, children are firmly convinced that 'the world is good'.

This is why lack of appetite and refusal to try something new is usually caused by some deeper reason, possibly more psychological in nature, and must be watched carefully. Certainly this indicates that life forces are impaired, which can come to expression in a particular organ – especially the stomach and liver – or in the relationship of children's whole bodies to their surroundings. The cause can be a single, weak, debilitated organ, or the result of psychological problems such as unhappiness, loneliness or anxiety.

In such cases we should be grateful if children want to tell us something is wrong, and it is better to observe them attentively to begin with than to take over-hasty measures to tackle the problem. It is certainly not a good idea to offer more things to eat and exert pressure. However, parents also need to distinguish between serious causes and superficial ones, such as: preferring to go and play; eating sweets before meals; or imitating the eating habits of siblings, other children or perhaps a parent who is dieting or fasting.

The evening meal and sleep

Why do young children often like eating re-heated food from lunchtime in the evening? Because their digestive organs already know the food in question. By evening, children – or at least their sensory organism – are tired and no longer have the energy to encounter, taste and digest something new. For this reason the evening meal should be simple and always similar to food eaten earlier in the day, or something children are already familiar with. Another golden rule for supper is: rich in carbohydrates, poor in fats and protein. Bread, grains, potatoes, vegetables, salads and fruit that is not too sour – sometimes cooked – are well tolerated, as are protein and fats contained in dairy products such as butter, cream, yoghurt and cottage cheese. Foods like hard or cooked cheese, eggs and meat, anything fried, or anything containing chemical additives such as phosphates can lead to restless sleep, night sweats, morning sluggishness or headaches and ultimately loss of appetite. This can make it hard to get up or wake up. Very sour fruits (citrus fruits, unripe fruit) or salad with vinegar, and in certain instances rice (which has a dehydrating effect) can act as diuretics in children and lead to disturbed sleep due to a full bladder. All such things can have direct repercussions on children's social behaviour and possibly their ability to concentrate.

The modern tendency to eat only snacks, fast foods, sweet things and light meals during the day, and then make up for this with a big evening meal, is understandable, but not a good idea even for adults, and completely unsuitable for children. Some adults only manage this with the help of an espresso, alcohol, medicines and then a coffee again in the morning, which is not an option for children!

Breakfast and energy

Reluctance to eat breakfast can be due to the evening meal the night before, or it can have a quite different cause. There are children whose blood sugar reserves in the liver are fully sufficient for coping with the first few hours of the day. One can see this in a child's ability to maintain attention until the next meal. Uncertainty or even anxiety about the day ahead can also make saliva and digestive juices dry up.

Children should certainly have something before they leave the house: milk, herb tea, grain or barley coffee, fruit juice, rusks, crispbreads, porridge, muesli, fruit and so on are all suitable. It is best if food is not too cold, is soft and fluid, and can be eaten in peace. Small quantities are enough. The digestion is now occupied, and any early vexations in the day will not fall on an empty stomach, which can sometimes lead to irritability and aggression.

In Germany, the real 'emperor's breakfast' comes between nine and ten o'clock, when the organ functions have woken up and are eager for action. The gall bladder, especially, wants to be active and needs the stimulus of hearty foods: fat and protein, fairly salty things in less easily digestible forms, such as hard or semi-hard cheeses, sausage, boiled or fried eggs, but also raw vegetables and wholemeal bread. In the UK, children have a lighter shared break mid-morning, consisting of a variety of healthy snacks, such as bread, fruit, muesli, rice pudding or soup.

If these important meals are missed there'll soon be tummy rumblings and reserves will be used up; children will become listless around midday, easily irritable, sluggish, and will clamour for sweet things. Sometimes they will no longer have the energy to eat a proper lunch. Eating and digesting take energy before they make more available again. Children then only want light, quick food, something familiar and undemanding and preferably 'alluring' in the way so skilfully presented today in packaging and advertising. Mother's lovingly prepared and healthy cooking seems powerless in the face of this.

A royal lunch

Arriving at the highpoint of the day, lunchtime, kindergarten-age children have been busy all morning but still have a lot to look forward to later in the day. They are hungry and need to recoup energy. The biggest meal of the day should address all the taste buds: sour (gives liveliness and cheerfulness), salty (strengthens bodily awareness), bitter (orders life forces) and sweet (I feel me in myself).

There can be a hint of *sourness* in salad dressing, though for younger children this should be less in the form of vinegar than lactic acid, such as yoghurt.

The modern diet tends not to include many *bitter* things, and only a delicate hint of this is needed in a young child's diet: using a bay leaf, juniper berries or a sage or tarragon leaf when cooking is sufficient to help cultivate a sure sense of when one is 'full'.

We feel something is missing from a meal if it has no *salty* constituent. A hearty vegetable soup is excellent as a precursor to rice pudding and fruit.

Sweetness in the form of carbohydrates is the meal's chief element: potatoes, noodles, any grain or the whole range of vegetables. These don't actually taste sweet – and if they did they would sate our appetite too quickly – but they are largely transformed into sugar in our bodies. By synthesising our own sugar we develop real strength (the word 'starch' is in fact derived from a Germanic word meaning 'strength'). The primary task of nutrition in the first seven years is to help children 'learn' and establish this process.

The types of grain served, and the forms they take, are all a question of preparation. Even 'indigestible' wholegrain rye can be cooked in an appetising way, whereas 'easily digested' white flour can become anything but due to processing and additives. It is important for food to look appealing and have a pleasant-sounding name, as do spaghetti and chips – far more so than an unsightly heap of wholegrains, however much one lauds them as being healthy and organically grown.

These two latter criteria should be of concern to the cook, but should not figure at the table: young children have a basic trust that whatever we give them to eat will be healthy and good, like breastmilk. All additional assurances that food is healthy tend to have a negative effect.

Young children love whatever has been prepared with pleasure and commitment for their personal needs. This is much more difficult when cooking for a group: here each child's needs are held back a little for the sake of the greater whole.

The value of grains and vegetables lies in a wealth of constituents that have still not yet been fully researched, which exist in harmonious, well-balanced compounds. Each vegetable is not just a source of 'multivitamins' and 'multiminerals', but also an 'organic symphony'. Eating a wealth of vegetables, with all their tempting colours, smells and shapes, is now known to be important in preventive healthcare.

Lighter vegetables such as carrots, courgettes, cucumbers, fennel and broccoli should take pride of place in children's diets, but those which take a bit more care in cooking, such as beetroot and cabbage, should not be completely excluded. The same is true of the grains. A wide range of wholegrain products, some more and others less pre-processed, are appetising and can be prepared easily: bulgur wheat, couscous, polenta etc.

Noodles have their place, and are pre-processed to such a degree that they won't cause digestive problems even when barely chewed; they're very easy food and good for 'weary soldiers'! Potatoes should be cooked thoroughly (reheating them twice is a good idea) with good fats (butter, sunflower oil) and aromatic herbs (fennel, caraway, marjoram) and served as mashed potato, dumplings or in casseroles. They should not be served more often than other vegetables, otherwise they marginalise the grains that are so rich in organising light forces, minerals and roughage, and give children 'something to chew on'.

Do children need a pudding? This custom comes from an over-emphasis on eating meat and seeks to balance a possible lack of carbohydrates. A meal of grains and vegetables does not require it. In fact, sugar disrupts the digestion of wholegrains, and can lead to flatulence.

It is a very good idea to have a rest of some kind after a meal. This does not have to mean lying down or sleeping, but simply quiet time, including daydreaming, a gentle walk or quiet game.

Drinks – what, when and how much?

Sweet drinks before meals can easily spoil children's appetite. While sweet things spoil the appetite, sour and bitter ones stimulate it, so children can have non-carbonated drinks such as herb teas or diluted fruit juice or a mixture of both (small quantities and not too cold). A midday meal of salad, vegetables and grains usually has a high water content (eighty to ninety per cent) and does not need additional fluid. This does not apply to meals of bread, cheese, sausage, jam, fried or baked foods, microwaved meals or ready meals. The latter often contain a lot of salt, along with other salts and acids (preservatives and additives) that increase the need for fluid. Drinking with meals impairs the flow of saliva and digestive juices.

When children say they are thirsty this is usually a physical need based on true perception. But parents and carers must decide themselves how best to quench children's thirst at a particular age. Children can only ask for what they know, have had on other occasions or see others having.

Thirst can also be the expression of a psychological need. This is especially apparent in children who can't fall asleep, who may be worried about something and want to 'drink' our attention.

Thirst is a primary physiological perception and should not be governed by others. Healthy children drink as much as they need; a kindergarten child may easily drink a litre of fluid a day.

Snacks and sweets

Young children have small stomachs and cannot assimilate large quantities of food at any one time. The needs of the day's most energetic periods can be met with breakfast, a mid-morning second breakfast or snack, and a full lunch.

However, even after an adequate, nutritious lunch, both children and adults can experience the desire for something sweet, light or tasty between two and three in the afternoon. Neither an apple nor wholemeal bread will satisfy this need. Liver activity leads blood sugar levels to fall at this time of day, giving rise to initial signs of bodily and emotional tiredness – even though there's still lots we want to do!

A short break and pause for reflection is a very good idea at this point. We don't need to fill ourselves up, but instead take pleasure in something lovingly prepared that melts in the mouth; something we can absorb with all our senses and soul – such as cake, biscuits, chocolate, cream, cocoa, coffee, tea, in pretty crockery and, best of all, accompanied by music or friendly conversation.

Gifts and sweet treats (perhaps saved from festivals) can now make their welcome appearance. A little pause in the ordinary, sometimes hectic, course of the day can allow space for refreshment of soul and spirit. Even the youngest children can enjoy a small princely feast!

Arranging a short mid-afternoon break has often proven its worth in quietening otherwise often-insistent demands for sweets. Enjoyment – of course not just physical in nature – is part of being human. We enjoy things with all our senses, which are largely located in the head and are closely related to our waking consciousness and alertness. In physiological terms, blood sugar is the basis of our alert awareness, endowing us with an 'innocent egotism' (Rudolf Steiner). Whenever we ask children to activate their senses and thinking, we encourage their urge for easily digestible carbohydrates, especially sugar. If, on the other hand, young children are allowed to dream and dwell peacefully in their own world, without their intellectual or rational faculties being called upon, this need for sweet things fades or doesn't arise so strongly in the first place. However paradoxical it sounds, giving children an intellectual explanation about tooth decay will actually encourage them to consume sugar!

Raw or cooked?

Thorough chewing is necessary to properly assimilate raw root crops such as carrots or beetroot. Digestion starts with chewing, but young children cannot yet do this, nor should they. They first need molars capable of grinding and pulverising the cell walls of food, allowing saliva to start working on its constituents to transform carbohydrates into sugar. If this process does not begin in the mouth, it cannot be continued in the stomach. It then calls only on secretions of the pancreas, which can have consequences for the whole digestive system, particularly if foods rich in fats (above all saturated fatty acids), drinking lots of fluids (see above), or tiredness and stress are also making the digestion process difficult.

Does this mean that young children should not eat such things as raw carrots? On the contrary: chewing strengthens the whole jaw including gums and circulation; it induces saliva formation and offers healthy resilience to emerging teeth, ultimately involving the whole digestive musculature through to elimination. Pieces of undigested carrot can often be found in stools: while they have not been of any nutritional benefit, they have served as 'training'.

We should therefore remember, firstly, that raw root foods

(including most types of cabbage) will provide children with only a small amount of nutrients; that, secondly, children's bodies have to 'warm up' the food itself, which can be too much for children with a weak warmth organism; and that, thirdly, healthy children will ask for as many bread crusts and raw vegetables as are good for them, so we should offer these but not insist.

Alongside this 'practice diet' young children's metabolism needs foods that have been 'further ripened' and opened up by heat. Ripe fruits cannot really be thought of as 'raw' in the strict sense, since they have been 'cooked' by the sun's warmth.

Typical leaf salads, primarily lettuces, can be classified as lying on a scale somewhere between fruit and root.

Salts and spices

The custom of introducing infants to adult food at an early stage leads to a very high salt intake, and to familiarity with few but often very strong tastes. Primarily these are pepper, yeast extract and glutamate. These are not adapted to young children's very delicate sense of taste, informed initially by the slight sweetness of milk and neutral taste of grains.

Salt is not necessary at all to start with, and later only in a tiny quantity. The natural aromas of different fruits and vegetables are initially fully adequate as taste nuances. Sometimes even these are too strong (celery, endive, orange). Later, herbs such as dill, parsley, chives and marjoram can be added in small quantities. Some kitchen herbs, especially when dried, have a mildly healing action and can therefore be used to address particular ailments or weaknesses. Exotic spices such as curry, chilli, ginger, nutmeg and cinnamon should ideally not be introduced until children reach school age. Some of these spices have an anti-bacterial effect and are therefore incompatible with the development of the intestinal flora. Originating in hot countries, they are associated with quite different modes of life and nutrition.

Dried fruits and nuts

The long exposure to warmth involved in making dried fruits, followed by much chewing and salivating, mean that they are very valuable for growing children. Apples, pears and apricots are best. Nuts are also an important part of the diet, but here we need to distinguish carefully. Walnuts are a typical winter food and should be eaten primarily in that season. Hazelnuts stimulate neurosensory activity and the brain, and should therefore be avoided if a child is already very awake or too alert; an increase in allergies can indicate this. These nuts are excellent 'brain food' for school children and students. Peanuts are a leguminous crop and ripen below the earth's surface. Rich in protein and susceptible to mildew, they are best eaten roasted and salted. Almonds are an excellent supplement to dried fruits, in particular in a young child's diet. They belong to the rose species and have some similarities with breastmilk. Almond puree (made of shelled almonds to begin with, then later of unshelled almonds) can be added to porridge and fruit mash, and is also suitable as a light but nutritious snack between meals.

Meat, eggs and fish

For many centuries, meat, eggs and fish played only a small part in children's diets. This changed firstly in response to the deprivations of World War II and rationing, and secondly as a result of the surplus still continuing today. At the beginning of the twentieth century, the recommended maximum daily intake of protein for adults was 140 g (5 oz). At the time, Rudolf Steiner stated that such a high intake of protein would increase susceptibility to infections. Nowadays, the scientific community recommends 60 g (2 oz) protein per day (for a bodyweight of 70 kg, 154 lb), but this level includes a big 'safety margin'. Modern consumers in civilised countries tend to ignore this and eat around 100 g (3½ oz) of protein daily. The recommended daily intake for a four to seven-year-old is 0.9 g per kg of bodyweight. This would be 13.5 g (½ oz) of protein for a weight of 15 kg (33 lb). This quantity equals roughly 60 g (2 oz) of lean veal or 100 g (3½ oz) of low-fat curd cheese (quark).

Meat consumption today is recommended largely to ensure sufficient trace elements in the diet such as iron, or a single fatty acid – but this takes no account of the many other constituents, let alone the whole character, of a particular food. It is perfectly clear that healthy children can meet their protein needs entirely with a lacto-vegetarian diet (vegetables plus milk and dairy products). The anthroposophic view of nutrition regards this as the most appropriate diet for young children, though small quantities of meat, eggs and fish can be added.

When we take an animal's life to sustain our own, it is important to view this food with gratitude and loving respect. Milk is, of course, different in this sense from meat, poultry and fish, as the animal that provides it is cared for and kept alive. Despite some modern hostility to a diet centred on dairy products – milk, cream, butter, quark, yoghurt and cheese – it remains extremely valuable for children's nutrition, at least in Northern and Central European countries, and replacing it entirely with other foods would be very difficult indeed.

Buying organic?

As we know, our children are exposed to numerous forms of environmental stress that we often cannot protect them from, to more than a limited extent. But we are relatively free when buying food to purchase produce grown without the use of pesticides or artificial fertilisers. Such food has been shown to contain more nourishing or beneficial constituents, so it really is advisable to 'buy organic'.

Even if it were not possible to prove conclusively that

organic produce is more nourishing, our children's future will ultimately depend on promoting ecologically sound and human-scale agriculture, and respectful care of the environment.

The ritual of meal times

In Waldorf kindergartens, shared meals are important moments in the day. They are embedded in recurring rhythms, rituals and customs that give children a sense of security. In some kindergartens the main meals follow a set cycle: a repeating sequence of grains, each of which is served on a particular day of the week. Adults might think that having the same dish on the same day each week is very boring, but young children love habits and routine, and take pleasure in the fact that, say, Wednesday is millet day, or that oat muesli means it is Friday. These meals support children's developing sense of time.

Many children no longer witness cooking at home or participate in shared meals. In kindergarten they not only benefit from the nutritional value of the foods served, but also enjoy the communal eating experience. They are likewise involved in the process of preparing each meal, learning to see how cooking and preparation is done. Some children spread butter on bread while others slice carrots or apples. There may be cake dough to stir for a tasty dessert, or bread dough to knead. The table needs laying too, and when children are old enough they can clear dishes away, wash them and sweep the floor.

All the children take part, and enjoy a wide range of sensory impressions in the process, such as smelling, tasting, touching, feeling; and of course they love helping and cooking, and develop a good appetite for the coming meal. Table manners and learning to handle spoons, knives and forks, also goes more smoothly when everyone learns together.

A shared meal develops all kinds of good habits and is not an unimportant extra. It provides a pause for tasting and enjoyment that every child can engage in. A grace to begin with and thanks at the end not only provide an outer framework to the meal, but also raise it out of the humdrum business of the day.

It will be clear, hopefully, that nurturing our children's healthy development and joyous participation in life is inseparable from their developing respect for all the living plants and creatures that provide our food; for the earth as a whole, too, with its water, air, light and warmth; and also for the people who grow, sell, prepare, cook and consume the produce.

The Importance of Parent Collaboration

Claudia Grah-Wittich

Our children are the future. The younger children are, the more intimately their thinking and lives are bound up with their immediate surroundings, in particular their parents. Children – especially infants – must always be seen in connection with their parents or key attachment figures. Changing circumstances and societal norms, along with parents' increasing desire to have fulfilling careers, mean that in Germany around twenty per cent of children under three, and almost 92 per cent of those under five, are cared for in nurseries and childcare facilities. A third of these receive whole-day care. Increasingly, diverse childcare facilities partly adopt this role too. Parents, however, remain the most important attachment figures for their children, even if they are mainly cared for by others during the day.

The legal right to childcare for all children up to three, which will come into force in Germany from August 2013, and will have cost the state billions of euros to implement, is leading to universally available facilities for the youngest babies in nurseries as well as additional groups in kindergartens and childcare centres. Soon after birth, therefore, parents and childcare professionals working with parents face a quite new question: how should parents and childcare professionals collaborate during this vital period of a child's life? How do we engage with each other – parents as primary attachment figures on the one hand, and professionally trained carers on the other? The rapid social changes underway mean that work with parents is assuming ever more important dimensions.

Early childhood development is of unique importance. Anthroposophic views accord with the latest scientific findings, regarding the early years, and especially the first three years, as decisive for our entire lives and as a period when our future potential is configured for good or ill. For example, *how* we learn to walk, speak and think, and how our bodily organism shapes itself overall, is of vital importance to our future autonomy.

Children mirror their surroundings

As adults we quickly notice how malleable and open young children are, and how they imitate not just our actions, but also absorb our feelings and thoughts. Their perceptions are immersed in and merged with their surroundings. The following can illustrate this: a father asks his wife in the evening how their son's day at nursery went, and the mother describes what was going on when she collected him. The three-year-old boy, apparently not involved at all in the conversation, but playing with his toy lorry, is in fact picking up everything and notices that, 'Mummy doesn't like Mrs so-and-so'.

Children, especially under the age of three – before they are able to detach themselves from the world through self-awareness – are entirely open and vulnerable to their surroundings. Even if children do not immediately show this, but instead absorb impressions inwardly, we must bear in mind how our relationship with the world affects our children; it has a strong effect on children's subsequent engagement with their social surroundings and their social integrity. The way parents and childcare work together is of great importance here.

In infant pedagogy, therefore, self-education and self-reflection will become an ever-more important aspect of dialogue between parents and childcare professionals, and should increasingly be accentuated in training courses as a developmental challenge for parents and carers.

A change of paradigm is becoming discernible. Alongside questions of educational practice and child development, attention is increasingly being drawn to the adult carer as the child's primary 'environment'. Pausing to become aware of our own responsibility in this respect provides a moment of freedom in changing our ingrained forms of behaviour. If we are to set an example, we have to 'put our own house in order' first. If I nurture feelings of attentiveness and respect, I foster my interest in a situation and, where necessary, in the different outlook of another person. This is the inner basis for working with parents and for inviting parents to collaborate with Steiner-Waldorf institutions.

Attachment figures

Numerous studies on attachment carried out since the seventies – most recently confirmed by findings in neurology and brain research – tell us that secure emotional attachment to at least one parent is the starting point for a child's development and capacity to feel at home in and engage with the world. As research and practice show, where nursery provision and acclimatisation are managed in the right way, an additional key attachment figure is certainly possible. In many situations this is necessary for children and even beneficial.

In a childcare facility, emotional attachment develops less through personal and emotional contact with a carer than through the latter's quality of competence and intentional engagement with children. This learned 'role' of caring is one that children perceive at the same time as absorbing their surroundings and atmosphere. They sense it in the attentive respect they receive and, above all, through actual tending. As long as the carer's attentive professional stance is maintained, children develop an attachment to carers as parent 'representatives', but parents always retain their status as such. This is a general and absolute requirement of quality childcare.

Repeatedly we can observe how, via the key attachment person, children will find great security and attachment in the premises themselves, and the rhythmic, meaningful daily routine. They will also perceive subliminally, but very accurately, how their mother or father feels about their care and the atmosphere there – and will take their lead from this.

Drama at hometime

Besides working with children, childcare facilities must adopt and develop a professional stance towards parents. The latter often feel at sea, and cope poorly with early separation from their children. It is necessary for children's well-being to include parents by developing a trusting relationship and supporting them. Describing what happens at hometime can give an insight into this.

When a mother arrives after a tiring and stressful day at work, her child will try to regain her emotional attention. This can be through various reactions such as smiling, crying, clinging to her or withdrawal, and is often misunderstood by the parent. Reactions like this often elicit feelings of anxiety and guilt, and dismissing such feelings helps neither the parent nor the child.

Here carers have an important bridging or mediating function, requiring much presence of mind and empathy. At such a moment they could, for instance, convey the child's needs to the parent in a few words and reassure her that this is a natural response and that nothing is wrong. This moment of handover often determines the nature of the brief remainder of the day for parents and children. The parents' bad conscience at having left their child may encourage the child to take the emotional reins until bedtime, demanding this or that treat or privilege and leaving parents helplessly entangled in their emotions.

Every meeting is a first encounter

Such transitional moments are important in childcare, and all parties involved need to communicate sensitively. This collaboration with parents will need to find its due place in future training courses for carers and teachers, paying particular attention to the perception of subtle signals that can reverberate long afterwards.

We all need to develop an 'organ' for attentive engagement and dialogue with each other, so that this becomes a real skill. Here we need to regard every human encounter as unique, occurring in a unique, situation-specific way. Every meeting is a first encounter! If this does not happen, the other person will not feel understood. As the American psychologist Winnicott saw it, this sense of being understood is of great importance for children: 'I am perceived therefore I am.' I am perceived *as* I am, and thus I am understood. Working continually on this inner stance is extremely valuable for collaboration between parents and childcare professionals.

Two worlds: home and childcare

The differences between home and childcare in terms of values, customs and impressions (smells, colours, atmosphere, family and religious culture, language etc.) can sometimes be very great and apparently unbridgeable. What might otherwise be fuel for conflict, however, can be handled in a conscious, loving way and instead become meaningful and complementary, benefitting the child. Given respectful dialogue, parents and carers can learn a great deal from each other. On the one hand, parents can bring all kinds of life experience to bear, and on other hand, they may be in a profession that has no connection with education and sometimes be at risk of losing sight of innate parenting skills.

The following diagram illustrates the relationship between parents and childcare facilities, and the potential problems it involves:

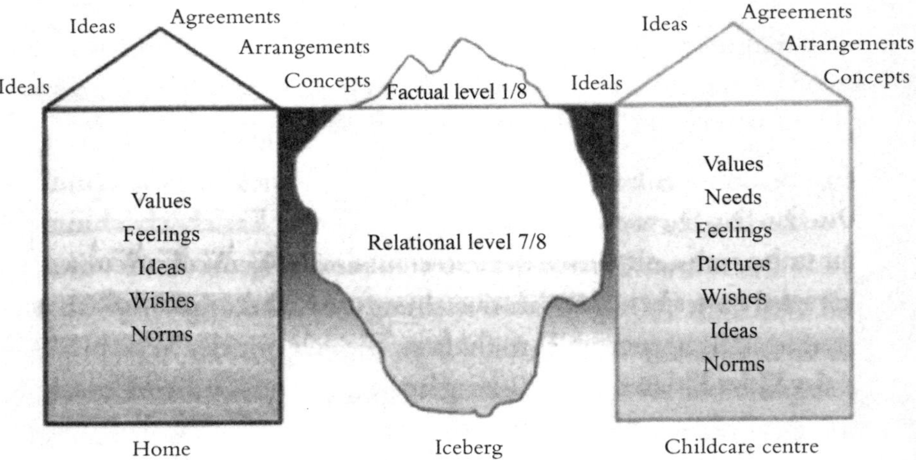

The diagram draws on the 'iceberg' metaphor current in psychology to characterise the relationship between home and childcare. The main mass of the iceberg (seven eighths) is below water, and likewise relationships between home and childcare play out largely in a subliminal realm 'below the surface'. Usually, for instance, the dialogue is largely factual, rather than discussing the far more important level of relationships and feelings.

Formal agreements are usually signed by parents and childcare centres, alongside many possible verbal arrangements. In the best scenario there is agreement about common ideals and educational outlooks, but this section constitutes only around one eighth of the real relationship. The greater part of the emotional connection – the seven eighths of the iceberg – occurs unconsciously. Here feelings, needs, values, norms, pictures and energy play an important role. This realm often goes neglected because it is not consciously noticed. If awareness of it is not raised, worked through and communicated, but instead suppressed, it can cause conflict between adults, and therefore impair children's psychosocial development.

Carers' needs, feelings and values do not necessarily accord with those of parents. If there is an unconscious expectation of this, it will lead to disappointment, a sense of hurt and subsequently to double messages. If we are aware of the diversity of the levels below the surface, we can better see how such messages are attributable to our own personalities and that of others.

Further training courses in parent-carer dialogue, and practical insight into principles such as 'nonviolent communication' as conceived by M. Rosenberg, can help and support all adults involved.[71] If parents and carers – each from their own context and outlook – let children know that all is well, young children can experience new, appropriate things in each 'system', and use both protected spaces for their own development.

Drawing on insights of the psychologist Michael Lukas Moeller, we could formulate the following principle for kindergarten and early years care: I cannot change the child's home or either of the parents. Even if this were possible I ought not to, for this would be a violation of their human rights. What I can do instead is to change my own points of view and outlook. If I am lucky this will alter the relationship.

For collaboration with parents, these principles mean the following:

- Learning to reflect on our own behaviour, often informed by our own ideas and outlook.
- Repeatedly practising awareness of emotional perceptions and feelings, and communicating them.
- Trying to stay centred and not imposing our own ideas on others.

If this approach is practised by responsible staff and managers, parents will also find it easier to be open minded and to stay centred in their parental role: taking responsibility for themselves, sharing their thoughts and feelings about their child and the care centre, and incorporating these in shared responsibility for the child's well-being.

Different levels of collaboration with parents

We can distinguish three levels of parental involvement:

1. Parent or family education, via courses and seminars
2. Parent participation
3. Parent counselling

Given the hundreds of published 'parenting manuals' available today, the first level, that of parent education, should not involve just adding to this wealth of advice. It is increasingly important to develop skills that enable parents to find their own unique 'family culture' and way of relating to their children, which means forming one's own views and judgements and determining where one's own boundaries lie. Here Waldorf education offers an enormous number of insights and suggestions, but should never be misunderstood as a normative 'lifestyle'.

Every form of parent collaboration depends, in general, on the inner stance of the childcare professional towards the parents, and on the latter's willingness to engage with new ideas. Let us consider this in more detail in relation to parent participation.

Parent participation

Parent participation means active partnership and collaboration in the care and education of children. In this process, parents wish to be included and taken seriously. If childcare is seen in the broadest sense as educational work, this assigns new value to the communal processes of organising festivals, renovating childcare premises, gardening and structural, organisational or financial involvement. Open and useful dialogue can become possible here by drawing on parents' particular professional skills, where appropriate. Experience has shown, though, that this requires healthy self-awareness on the part of carers or teachers.

To enable parent participation to succeed, childcare professionals need to develop three skills:

1. Taking responsibility for shared processes
2. Self-reflection and self-examination
3. Conscious development of their own stance and outlook

In an era when, increasingly, both parents are working, or a lone parent is bringing up children, we can assume that they will have less time to be actively involved in practical forms of support. Parents who entrust their child to care need to use their remaining time for family life and leisure time. If a childcare centre starts from this premise it will not have false expectations or demands, which may lead to disappointment and tension between parents and staff.

Parents' evenings

Parents' evenings offer a space for meeting and dialogue. At nurseries where both parents are predominantly in full-time work, attendance at such evenings may sometimes be poor. Here, too, we must consider the family's needs. On the one hand, they will be very interested to hear accounts of their children's progress and the philosophy of the childcare centre, but their primary need will be for respite and relaxation. This requires a selfless approach from staff, and good internal dialogue in the childcare team to engage with all resulting issues. Parents' evenings should be held as often as necessary and as infrequently as possible, always oriented to parents' needs. How they are organised offers a good opportunity for practising the inner stance outlined above, with open dialogue and real encounter to serve each child's best interests. It has repeatedly been found that themes come to life much better and have more lasting benefit through practical activities and exercises rather than just discussions or talks. The common basis and shared experiences they develop nurture community life and provide first-hand insights into the childcare centre's educational approach.

Taking responsibility

Responsibility for constructive collaboration falls in the first instance to childcare professionals, who need to actively shape the relationship with parents, for they are in a leadership position. Arbitrary actions, for example without understandable basis or motives, or ambiguous messages, make parents uncertain. Initially parents may tolerate such conduct since they rely on kindergarten teachers and depend on their child having a place at the centre. But the mood and level of commitment will suffer. Taking responsibility for parents' meaningful participation represents a great additional challenge for carers, kindergarten teachers and the institution as a whole.

In the daily life of a childcare centre, the same arguments repeatedly surface as apparently good grounds for impeding constructive collaboration:

- 'I have no time.'
- 'I don't have the skills for this and feel too much is being asked of me.'
- 'Unfortunately we don't have the money for this.'
- 'Parents always want to have a say without actually helping.'
- 'Parents understand too little about our educational approach.'

Childcare professionals must overcome these understandable gestures of self-defence by taking conscious responsibility for work with parents. Parents should bring their own skills and life experiences to this process, engaging in dialogue and partnership, and sharing their observations and feelings.

Self-reflection and self-examination

If childcare professionals desire greater parent participation, or wish to alter something in an existing process or relationship, they must first examine themselves rather than blaming external factors, as all too easily happens. In educational professionalism, everyone is his or her own 'first educator'. Am I aware of my own stance towards the parents? Do I respect them, despite them having such a different outlook? Good intentions alone are not enough. The important thing is how I convey them and actually communicate. Being aware of this is the first important step in self-reflection.

It is common for our own vulnerabilities or lack of self-awareness to hinder our open engagement with parents. This is the 'large section of iceberg below the water', consisting of anxieties, expectations, needs and values – our unresolved areas that are often unconscious. Psychologist Eric Bernes describes these as the 'child level', co-existing with the 'parent level' and the 'partner level'.[72]

Our vulnerabilities and feelings bring out the 'inner child' in us: a realm in which we behave like a three-year-old having a tantrum, or a sullen adolescent. Such conduct calls forth the 'parent ego' in another person, and where these two elements collide, the seeds of conflict are sown. In such situations it is very helpful to discover what 'level' we are acting from, and seek instead for a collaborative level with the other person.

We engage lovingly and sympathetically with sad or angry children, and we must direct this empathic attentiveness towards ourselves too, parallel to increasing individualisation. In self-reflective observation we need to be aware of these subtle aspects of the psyche, and learn to communicate them. Outer obstacles, resistance or disappointment can best be seen as important impetus and opportunities for our further self-development. So often what seems to arise from our surroundings is in fact intimately connected with ourselves.

Through specific exercises, anthroposophy offers a path for consciously working on our own personality. We can start this whenever we wish to reflect on our own thinking, feeling and actions. Straightforward mindfulness exercises show how difficult it is to stay centred and dwell in a focused, contemplative or meditative frame of mind, but we should make this the basis of our actions. Educators and childcare professionals can lead by example here.[73]

Our inner stance is all-important

Qualities that support our emotional awareness are vital for successful parent participation – especially for childcare professionals seeking to lead by example. Such qualities are:

1. Being inwardly present and attentive
2. Being authentic or congruent
3. Valuing the other person
4. Communicating empathically

1. Being inwardly present and attentive

Being inwardly present and attentive is needed for real human encounter to thrive. By contrast, anxiety, uncertainty and vulnerability quickly lead to avoidance of direct contact: if we are preoccupied with our own fears, we are not sufficiently available to the other person. Unconscious entanglement in our own concerns will often raise defensive barriers. Courage is required if we are to be open in every moment, allowing us to lower our defences and engage directly in the encounter.

2. Being authentic or congruent

Another person will immediately notice whether our words or actions are in harmony with our thoughts and feelings. An apparently objective matter may not be properly understood, even when conveyed in the friendliest manner, if annoyance, anger or grief is present in the background. Either we manage to overcome our feelings, or we discuss them honestly. This makes space for the other's understanding.

3. Valuing the other person

In every collaborative situation, mistakes are made and *are allowed* to be made. The important thing is to remain in dialogue. Everyone notices immediately if they and their work are valued, quite irrespective of mistakes or differences of opinion. This is extremely important for free interaction. Esteem is always accorded to people rather than to their behaviour in a particular instance.

4. Communicating empathically

The basis for empathy towards others is a capacity to be centred in oneself and authentic. If we are really centred and present in ourselves, we can engage with others and show genuine sympathy, interest and appreciation. This gives rise quite naturally to empathic communication: perceiving and attending to other people's needs and comments without projecting our own thoughts and ideas on them.

Cultivating the above qualities, and conscious engagement with or even just reflection on our own behaviour, will positively affect each relationship between parents and childcare professionals. These qualities also play a key role today in *parent education* and *parent counselling*, and are vital in responsible practice of the art of education.

Qualities of parent counselling

Parent counselling in the sense intended here is additional to childcare professionals' daily work. It involves giving qualified advice where problems of upbringing and education arise, and holding discussions relating to pedagogical issues that are causing parents distress. What qualities does a counsellor need to develop to meet this widespread need of parents – or even, sometimes, to deal with emergencies? Are childcare professional aware of their own limitations – of the point at which other professionals should be involved or at which they themselves need further training to meet this challenge?

Sometimes just a quick piece of advice in passing can be very helpful. But usually one has to understand the whole context and situation to deal with even a small issue. An answer to a problem parents have will often lie concealed in the very question they ask. It is often a matter of finding the answer that people carry within them, and making it visible and tangible. The aim of a counselling session is to formulate the 'advice' in a way that simply reflects what has been said by both parties. This not only enlarges parents' sense of their own capacities, but highlights a path whereby parents can increasingly come to trust themselves, taking responsibility for themselves and their own aims. By contrast, prescriptive formulations create dependency and a hierarchical system within the childcare centre that should be avoided at all costs.

Quality discussions with parents require considerable time and inner space, as well as a suitable room, and there is usually only limited opportunity for this in the normal framework of a childcare facility. It is, therefore, a good idea to develop additional counselling facilities if appropriate, or to collaborate with a suitable educational advice service or early years support team. But before embarking on this process it is important to gain the consent and agreement of parents as a first step.

What happens in a counselling session of this kind, and how can parents get the help they are looking for?

Those who wish to practise counselling, over and above their work with children and parents, need specialist knowledge and a set of tried and tested tools. The counselling session itself might be compared with a sort of 'meditative detective work'. First we must free our minds by reflecting on all our first – often important – impressions, registering our judgements and prejudices. Then we must establish a basis of trust, a sense of warmth and well-being.

This *warm-up* phase is followed by *establishing the full picture*: illuminating any 'dark corners', bringing to light as many aspects of the situation as possible without judging. Empathic and attentive listening will often allow more to emerge than the counsellor initially expected. Up to this point there can be no judging or prejudging of the situation, nor of course any over-hasty solution. There should be freedom to express everything and anything. Questions put by the counsellor support this process, as does the method of simply recapitulating what has been said in one's own words.

In the next phase, that of *structuring*, key areas can be elaborated and formulated. It is important to establish a mood of shared work, to discover the solution that lies within the person being counselled; by holding back their own views, counsellors, rather like detectives, seek to discover the appropriate steps for the other person to take. This requires a high level of concentration and focus, to maintain empathic interest in the other party. The themes that surface can be identified and explored to see whether the other person also regards them as important. Any decision always lies with the other party.

Only in the *concluding* phase can the discussion culminate in a summary and agreement. Issues that cannot be properly dealt with 'in passing', and are left unresolved because of insufficient time, can here be calmly explored in depth. It no longer matters if the participants started from very different premises; an inner, collaborative process is set in motion if this 'space for discussion' develops in the right way.

Building bridges

The quality of counselling sessions and of parent work in general lies in respect between adults, of a kind that should also be self-evident in our attitude towards children. This builds bridges between the childcare centre and the family's world, founded on the mutual stance of all those involved. Working relationships thrive best on the basis of consciously handled human collaboration. 'The fundamental maxim of the free individual,' says Rudolf Steiner, 'is to live with love for one's own actions and with respect and understanding for the intentions of others.'[74]

Endnotes

1. See Steiner, *The Education of the Child.*
2. See for instance: Carlgren & Klingborg, *Education Towards Freedom.*
3. Steiner, comments on June 23, 1920 and December 21, 1921.
4. See Puhani & Weber, 'Does the Early Bird Catch the Worm?' The full study can be downloaded from the internet at: ftp://ftp.iza.org/dps/dp1827.pdf (English version).
5. See Paul, *Levana or the Doctrine of Education.*
6. See Schaefer (ed.), *Bildung beginnt mit der Geburt.*
7. See Neall, *Bringing the Best Out in Boys.*
8. See Beck, *Risikogesellschaft* (also published in English as *Risk Society*).
9. See Maslow, *Toward a Psychology of Being.*
10. See Maslow, *Motivation and Personality.*
11. See Schiffer, *Wie Gesundheit entsteht.*
12. Cited in Schiffer, as above.
13. See Marti, *Wie kann Schule die Gesundheit fördern?*
14. See Aeppli, *The Care and Development of the Human Senses*; Soesman, *The Twelve Senses.*
15. See Steiner, *The Education of the Child.*
16. Ibid.
17. See Hüther, *Männer.*
18. See Spitzer, *Lernen.*
19. See Schoeler, Keilmann, Heinemann, Schakib-Ekbatan, *Biographische und anamnestische Informationen.*
20. See Steiner, *The Education of the Child.*
21. See Stern, *Psychologie der frühen Kindheit.*
22. See Steiner, *Verses and Meditations.*
23. See Steiner, *The Education of the Child.*
24. See Steiner and Wegman, *Fundamentals of Therapy.*
25. See Largo, *Kinderjahre.*
26. Ibid.

27. Pikler, *Friedliche Babys, zufriedene Mütter*, p. 73.
28. The concept of the Waldorf kindergarten with mixed age groups was based on an idea of 'kindergarten readiness' comparable to 'school readiness'.
29. I worked on this theme for my doctorate in early years education completed in 1983, under the title of: 'The child's first three years – approaches to working with parents', comparing comments by Rudolf Steiner with those of Emmi Pikler.
30. See Patzlaff et al., *The Child from Birth to Three in Waldorf Education and Childcare.*
31. See Steiner, *The Education of the Child.*
32. See Steiner, *Soul Economy and Waldorf Education*, lecture of December 29, 1921; and Lievegoed, *Phases of Childhood.*
33. Drawings by Robert Neumann.
34. See Steiner, *The Education of the Child.*
35. Ibid.
36. See Steiner, *Soul Economy and Waldorf Education* (GA 303).
37. Further reading on festivals: Jaffke, *Celebrating Festivals with Children*; Barz, *Festivals with Children.*
38. See Steiner, *The Child's Changing Consciousness and Waldorf Education*, GA 306, lecture 4.
39. See Jaffke, *Toymaking with Children.*
40. See Jaffke, *Celebrating Festivals with Children.*
41. See Jaffke, *Work and Play in Early Childhood.*
42. See Steiner, *The Education of the Child.*
43. See Ellersiek, *Dancing Hand, Trotting Pony.*
44. Ibid.
45. Ibid.
46. Ibid.
47. Source: www.teachersnews.net
48. See the research results compiled by partners in the 'Alliance for Childhood', www.allianceforchildhood.org
49. Wilson, *The Hand.*
50. See for instance, Grossman and DeGaetano, *Stop Teaching Our Kids to Kill.*
51. See Patzlaff (ed.), 'Kindheit verstummt'.
52. See Ellersiek, *Dancing Hand, Trotting Pony* and *Giving Love – Bringing Joy.*
53. Ellersiek, *Dancing Hand, Trotting Pony*, p.14.
54. Ibid., pp.13–14.
55. Ibid., p.14.
56. See Ellersiek, *Giving Love – Bringing Joy.*
57. See books by Ellersiek, published by WECAN, some of which

are mentioned in previous notes; see also Matterson, *This Little Puffin.*

58. Esterl, *Die Märchenleiter*, p.25f.
59. You will find some lovely short stories for reading aloud in Lockie, *Bedtime Storytelling.*
60. Interview in *Spiegel* magazine, 45/2007.
61. For example, Ellersiek, *Giving Love – Bringing Joy*, and the CD of same title.
62. See Kreusch-Jacob, *Jedes Kind braucht Musik.* The book contains a wealth of music and movement games.
63. These instruments are available from www.myriadonline.co.uk
64. Juergen Knothe in *waldorf-hessen*, no. 11, October 2006.
65. Schiffer, *Der kleine Prinz in Las Vegas*, p.8.
66. See Jaffke, *Work and Play in Early Childhood*; Neuschütz, *Children's Creative Play*; Jaffke, *On the Play of the Child*; Long-Breipohl, *Supporting Self-directed Play in Steiner-Waldorf Early Childhood Education.*
67. Spitzer, *Lernen*, p. 225.
68. See Piaget, *The Language and Thought of the Child*; and Piaget and Inhelder, *Psychology of the Child.*
69. See Large, *Set Free Childhood*; Stoll, *High Tech Heretic.*
70. See, for example, Grossman and DeGaetano, *Stop Teaching Our Kids to Kill.*
71. See Rosenberg, *Nonviolent Communication.*
72. See Berne, *Transactional Analysis in Psychotherapy.*
73. See Steiner, *Six Steps in Self-Development.*
74. See Steiner, *The Philosophy of Freedom*, GA 4, Chapter IX: 'The idea of Freedom'.

Bibliography

Aeppli, Willi. *The Care and Development of the Human Senses: Rudolf Steiner's Work on the Significance of the Senses in Education.* Floris Books, 2013.

Barz, Brigitte. *Festivals with Children.* Floris Books, 1987.

Beck, Ulrich. *Risikogesellschaft. Auf dem Weg in eine andere Moderne.* Frankfurt/M. 1986. Published in English as *Risk Society: Towards a New Modernity.* Sage, 1992.

Berne, Eric. *Transactional Analysis in Psychotherapy.* Eigal Meirovich, 2009.

Carlgren, Frans and Arne Klingborg. *Education Towards Freedom.* Floris Books, 2008.

Ellersiek, Wilma. *Dancing Hand, Trotting Pony: Hand Gesture Games, Songs and Movement Games for Children in Kindergarten and the Lower Grades.* WECAN, 2010.

—, *Giving Love – Bringing Joy: Hand Gesture Games and Lullabies in the Mood of the Fifth, for Children Between Birth and Nine.* WECAN, 2003.

Esterl, Arnica. *Die Märchenleiter.* Verlag Freies Geistesleben 2007.

Grossman, D. and Gloria DeGaetano. *Stop Teaching Our Kids to Kill: A Call to Action against TV, Movie and Video Game Violence.* Crown Publications, 1999.

Hüther, Gerald. *Männer. Das schwache Geschlecht und sein Gehirn.* Göttingen, 2009.

Jaffke, Freya. *Celebrating Festivals with Children.* Floris Books, 2011.

—, *On the Play of the Child: Indications by Rudolf Steiner for Working with Young Children.* WECAN, 2013.

—, *Toymaking with Children.* Floris Books, 2010.

—, *Work and Play in Early Childhood.* Floris Books, 1996.

Kreusch-Jacob, Dorothée. *Jedes Kind braucht Musik.* Munich, 2006.

Large, Martin. *Set Free Childhood: Parents' Survival Guide for Coping with Computers and TV.* Hawthorn Press, 2003.

Largo, Remo H. *Kinderjahre: Die Individualität des Kindes als erzieherische Herausforderung.* Munich, 2009.

Lievegoed, Bernard. *Phases of Childhood*. Floris Books, 2005.
Lockie, Beatrys. *Bedtime Storytelling: A Collection for Parents*. Floris Books, 2010.
Long-Breipohl, Renate. *Supporting Self-directed Play in Steiner-Waldorf Early Childhood Education*. WECAN, 2010.
Marti, Thomas. *Wie kann Schule die Gesundheit fördern? Erziehungskunst und Salutogenese*. Stuttgart, 2006.
Maslow, Abraham Harold. *Toward a Psychology of Being*. Princeton, 1962.
—, *Motivation and Personality*. Pearson, 1997.
Matterson, Elizabeth. *This Little Puffin: A Treasury of Nursery Rhymes, Songs and Games*. Puffin, 1991.
Neall, Lucinda. *Bringing the Best Out in Boys*. Hawthorn Press, 2003.
Neuschütz, Karin. *Children's Creative Play: How Simple Dolls and Toys Help Your Child Develop*. Floris Books, 2013.
Patzlaff, Rainer (ed.). 'Kindheit verstummt'. In *Luftlautformen sichtbar gemacht. Sprache als plastische Gestaltung der Luft*. Stuttgart, 2003.
Patzlaff, Rainer et al. *The Child from Birth to Three in Waldorf Education and Childcare*. Floris Books, 2011.
Paul, Jean. *Levana or the Doctrine of Education*. Ulan Press, 2012.
Piaget, Jean. *The Language and Thought of the Child*. Routledge, 2001.
Piaget, Jean and Baerbel Inhelder. *Psychology of the Child*. Routledge, 1969.
Pikler, Emmi. *Friedliche Babys, zufriedene Mütter*. Freiburg, 2000.
Puhani, Patrick A. and Andrea M. Weber. 'Does the Early Bird Catch the Worm? Instrumental Variable Estimates of Educational Effects of Age of School Entry in Germany'. TU Darmstadt. Nov. 2005.
Rosenberg, Marshall. *Nonviolent Communication*. Puddledancer Press, 2003.
Schaefer, Gerd (ed.). *Bildung beginnt mit der Geburt. Ein offener Bildungsplan für Kindertageseinrichtungen in Nordrhein-Westfalen*. Berlin, 2007.
Schiffer, Eckhard. *Der kleine Prinz in Las Vegas. Mit spielerischer Intelligenz den Herausforderungen unserer Zeit begegnen*. Weinheim, 1997.
—, *Wie Gesundheit entsteht. Salutogenese: Schatzsuche statt Fehlerfahndung*. Weinheim/Basel, 2001.
Schoeler, H, A. Keilmann, M. Heinemann and K. Schakib-Ekbatan. *Biographische und anamnestische Informationen sowie sprachliche und nichtsprachliche Leistungen bei 172 stationär behandelten schwer sprachentwicklungsgestörten Kindern. Eine Dokumentation*.

(Arbeitsberichte aus dem Forschungsprojekt 'Differentialdiagnostik', no. 12). Heidelberg: Pädagogische Hochschule, Institut für Sonderpädagogik, Abt. Psychologie in sonderpädagogische Handlungsfeldern.

Soesman, Albert. *The Twelve Senses: Introduction to Anthroposophy Based on Rudolf Steiner's Studies of the Senses*. Hawthorn Press, 1990.

Spitzer, Manfred. *Lernen. Gehirnforschung und die Schule des Lebens.* Heidelberg, 2002.

Steiner, Rudolf. *The Child's Changing Consciousness and Waldorf Education*. Anthroposophic Press, 1988.

—, *The Education of the Child*. Anthroposophic Press, 1996.

—, *The Philosophy of Freedom*. Rudolf Steiner Press, 2011.

—, *Six Steps in Self-Development*. Rudolf Steiner Press, 2010.

—, *Soul Economy and Waldorf Education*. Anthroposophic Press, 1986.

—, *Verses and Meditations*. Rudolf Steiner Press, 1961.

Steiner, Rudolf and Ita Wegman. *Fundamentals of Therapy: An Extension of the Art of Healing through Spiritual-Scientific Knowledge*. GA 27. Mercury Press, 2010.

Stern, William. *Psychologie der frühen Kindheit*. Heidelberg, 1967.

Stoll, Clifford. *High Tech Heretic: Why Computers Don't Belong in the Classroom and Other Reflections by a Computer Contrarian*. Bantam Doubleday Dell Publishing Group, 1999.

Wilson, Frank R. *The Hand: How its Use Shapes the Brain, Language, and Human Culture*. Vintage Books, 1999.

Useful Websites

Australia
Steiner Education Australia: www.steinereducation.edu.au

New Zealand
Federation of Rudolf Steiner Schools in New Zealand: www.rudolfsteinerfederation.org.nz

North America
Association of Waldorf Schools of North America (AWSNA): www.whywaldorfworks.org

Waldorf Early Childhood Association of North America (WECAN): www.waldorfearlychildhood.org

South Africa
South African Federation of Waldorf Schools: www.waldorf.org.za

UK
Steiner Waldorf Schools Fellowship (UK): www.steinerwaldorf.org.uk

International
International Association for Steiner-Waldorf Early Childhood Education (IASWECE): www.iaswece.org

About the Authors

Marie-Luise Compani is a Waldorf kindergarten teacher, and teaches further professional development courses at the Waldorf kindergarten training seminar in Stuttgart. She also regularly teaches in-service training courses in Eastern Europe and South Korea. A member of various committees within the Waldorf kindergarten movement, she supervises the setting up and development of Waldorf nursery facilities in Baden-Württemberg. A mother of three grown-up children, she lives in Stuttgart.

Elisabeth Göbel was born in Berlin. After experiencing the bombing of Berlin and its evacuation, she fled to Wendlingen/Teck in 1945 and from there attended the Stuttgart Waldorf School. She studied eurythmy and stagecraft from 1951. From 1956 she worked as a eurythmist in Dresden, before fleeing to the West in 1961. She is the mother of two children and since 1966 has worked as a eurythmist in Göttingen, initially giving courses and then working in kindergarten groups and subsequently teaching eurythmy at the Waldorf school. She has also given professional development training courses at Waldorf kindergarten seminars, and for eurythmists in Göttingen specialising in work with young children.

Claudia Grah-Wittich studied philosophy, art history and social work. She works in early years support and parent counselling at 'der hof' education and therapy centre in Frankfurt, and shares responsibility for the further training courses run there, as well as teaching courses around Germany and abroad. She is an advisor for the AKK (Waldorf kindergarten association working group) on setting up childcare facilities for the under-threes. She is married and the mother of three grown-up children.

Freya Jaffke is an experienced Waldorf kindergarten teacher. After working for many decades at the Waldorf kindergarten in Reutlingen, Germany, she taught on seminars in Germany and abroad. Numerous titles by her have been published in English by Floris Books.

Michael Kassner attended Waldorf schools in Rendsburg and Marburg, Germany. Subsequently he worked in curative education in England and Germany. For seven years he worked in biodynamic agriculture and gardening, and for twelve years at the 'Working group for nutritional research' in Bad Liebenzell, Germany. Since 1993 he has been a freelance advisor on nutrition and education, giving lectures and seminars across Europe. He teaches in adult education and is co-founder of the 'International Independent Seminar for Nutrition, Education and Dietetics' and tutor at the Waldorf kindergarten seminar in Stuttgart.

Birgit Krohmer is a Waldorf kindergarten teacher, eurythmist and eurythmy therapist. For many years she has also worked in training nursery carers, midwives, teachers and therapists both in Germany and abroad. She works as a professional advisor to Waldorf childcare centres and lives in Freiburg with her husband and three teenage children.

Peter Lang worked in business studies while training as an actor at Stuttgart's National Theatre. He studied youth and social work in Hanover and qualified as a social worker. For ten years he directed Freiburg's Youth and Culture Centre, and during this period qualified as a teacher at Freiburg College of Education. He was a lecturer at the School of Social Pedagogy and the College of Social Studies in Freiburg. In 1980/81 he attended the anthroposophical student seminar in Stuttgart, and from 1981 worked as a lecturer in education, psychology and Waldorf education on the Waldorf kindergarten seminar in Stuttgart, which he directed from 1983 to 2005. During this period he was an executive member of the Association of Waldorf Schools in Germany. From 1990 he worked as a lecturer and seminar supervisor in Korea, Lithuania, Ukraine and Turkey. He is an executive member of the Baden-Württemberg Association of Waldorf Kindergartens, has published numerous articles on education, and lectures widely.

Claudia McKeen is a GP and Waldorf kindergarten and school doctor. She lectures at the Waldorf kindergarten seminar in Stuttgart, giving training courses and further development courses for Waldorf nursery carers and kindergarten teachers. She is a member of the joint committees of the Waldorf kindergarten and school movement, which are concerned with collaboration between kindergartens and schools.

Andreas Neider is an author, editor, lecturer, journalist and freelance speaker on media issues in adolescent and adult education. He studied philosophy, ethnology, history and political science in Berlin. For seventeen years he worked at the anthroposophic publishing house Verlag Freies Geistesleben as editor and publisher. From 2002 he was director of the cultural agency 'Von Mensch zu Mensch' ('Person to Person'), managing anthroposophic events and educational conferences. Since 2007 he has worked as an author and lecturer in Waldorf kindergartens and schools, and in church and government educational institutes. He is a guest lecturer at Stuttgart Youth Seminar, and the editor of numerous publications for Verlag Freies Geistesleben.

Angelika Prange trained as a kindergarten teacher and founded a Waldorf kindergarten. After bringing up a family she worked as a lecturer at the College for Social Pedagogy in Stuttgart. Since 2000 she has worked at the kindergarten of the Stuttgart Waldorf School.

Jacqueline Walter-Baumgartner trained in Bern as a Waldorf Kindergarten teacher after a placement in a nursery and collaboration with a puppet theatre. She founded the Rudolf Steiner kindergarten in Rheinfelden, Switzerland, and has worked there since as group leader and practice manager. For eleven years she also managed the playgroup there, and from 1999 onwards the parent-child afternoon sessions. She has taught courses since 1989, primarily on rhythmic and musical hand gesture games and ring games, and on free play in the early years. From 1993 she taught regularly at the Rudolf Steiner kindergarten seminar in Bern. From 2005 to 2009 she was an executive member of the International Association for Steiner-Waldorf Early Childhood Education. She is a member of the international working group for rhythmic and musical hand gesture games, and is active in the Infant and Early Years Commission of Rudolf Steiner Kindergartens in Switzerland, and the Swiss branch of the Alliance for Childhood.

Related books

Work and Play in Early Childhood

Freya Jaffke

Rhythm and repetition, together with example and imitation, are pillars on which early learning is based. Freya Jaffke applies these simple principles in practical and sensible ways.

She describes children's play in a Steiner-Waldorf kindergarten setting, and provides tried and tested advice on this important stage of development.

www.florisbooks.co.uk

Children's Creative Play

How Simple Dolls and Toys Help Your Child Develop

Karin Neuschütz

Many parents find it hard to know which toys are appropriate for children at different ages, and what kinds of play to initiate and encourage. What can parents do to best help children develop, and foster their skills?

Karin Neuschütz, an experienced educator and parent, addresses these questions in this concise, readable book. She discusses how children play, creatively and freely, and how they are affected by their environment and by the adults near them.

She explores each developmental stage up to age seven, using case studies to illustrate particular issues. She then suggests suitable toys and dolls and nurturing activities for children at particular stages .

Understanding Waldorf Education

Teaching from the Inside Out

Karin Neuschütz

A jargon-free view of Waldorf education and its philosophy of a three-dimensional education.

Since their inception over 80 years ago, Steiner-Waldorf schools have offered a much-needed model for educational reform. The author provides a compelling, clearly written picture of the key components of a Waldorf education, focusing especially on child learning experiences that develop thought, feeling, and intentional, purposeful activity.

Ideal for parents, this book gives a common sense understanding of an education which answers modern needs in over one thousand schools across the world.

www.florisbooks.co.uk